LIFE WITH A MID-LIFE MAN

Your husband's mid-life crisis may cause you some of the greatest stress you have ever experienced.

- You will be shocked to see him question values and choices you thought had been settled long ago.
- You will have trouble understanding why he is so taken up with his aging.
- When he accuses you of being the cause of his problems or gives you the cold, silent treatment, you will feel rejected and misunderstood.

These may be anxious, confusing days for both of you. But if your husband successfully integrates the conflicts raging within him, a better life lies ahead.

As the wife of a mid-life husband you need to know some basic facts, the resources available to you, and what you can do to help your husband through this most difficult of times.

SALLY CONWAY has learned to juggle many different roles: pastor's wife, counselor, mother of three daughters, conference speaker, and university student. She and her husband, Jim, live in Urbana, Ill., where he is pastor of the 2,000-member Twin Cities Bible Church.

YOU AND YOUR HUSBAND'S MID LIFE CRISIS

Sally Conway

David C. Cook Publishing Co.

ELGIN, ILLINOIS—WESTON, ONTARIO

First printing, November 1980
Eighth printing, August 1984

YOU AND YOUR HUSBAND'S MID-LIFE CRISIS
© 1980 Sally Conway

Scripture quotations, unless otherwise noted, are from the Living Bible.

Published by David C. Cook Publishing Co.
850 N. Grove, Elgin, IL 60120
Printed in the United States of America

Library of Congress Cataloging in Publication Data

Conway, Sally.
    You and your husband's mid-life crisis.

    Includes bibliographical references.
    1. Climacteric, Male. 2. Menopause. I. Title.
RC884.c66   612'.665   80-23863
ISBN: 0-89191-318-1

To Jim,

*whose entire life as my husband
has been a living example
of the sacrificial love and
servanthood of Christ, and
whose mid-life storm taught us both
more about vulnerable living and loving*

CONTENTS

FOREWORD

For the past year and a half, a seemingly endless stream of telephone calls and letters have come to us from women all across the country. They usually begin by saying, "*Men in Mid-Life Crisis* describes my husband exactly. I was ready to give up on our marriage, but after reading the book I now understand that what is happening in my husband is something rather temporary."

The next comments usually describe their particular situation. Even though the names and places are different, again and again we have heard the same story of a husband struggling desperately with the meaning of life.

The major purpose of the woman who is writing or calling, however, is to ask, "How can I survive during this time? I understand that I need to meet my husband's needs, but who meets my needs?"

To those general questions are added specific ones, such as, "What do I tell the children?" "Should I force him to choose between me and his girl friend?" "How can I save our marriage?" "Should I move out of the house?" "Should I kick him out of the house?" "What should I tell our parents?" "How much should I change to please him?"

Sally and I have found ourselves spending hundreds of hours counseling through letters and long-distance telephone calls. Many times we answer the same questions we have just answered in previous letters or calls. This book, therefore, is an attempt to meet some of the needs and answer some of the questions of many women whose husbands are going through mid-life crises.

As we began to see a growing need for this book, Sally collected data through a nationwide survey that would help us to more fully understand the problems that women were experiencing and to learn some of their sources of strength. The information from this national survey, as well as information from personal correspondence and counseling, has been integrated into this book as real, live situations but with the names changed.

Sally Conway is a woman who has always been involved in leadership, from her high school days when she was class president and graduated valedictorian to her involvement in community organizations and in each of the churches I have pastored. She has been a public school teacher two different times; the last experience was as a remedial reading specialist.

In recent years she has taken on a new career of editing and writing. She has also been thrust into the role of conference speaker because of her deep interest in child development, marriage and family, Christian womanhood, and the mid-life crisis.

In spite of Sally's ever-expanding leadership role and changing career directions, she has continued to be sought after by younger women who want to know how she has been able to be such an effective mother to our three daughters, wife to me, and pastor's wife to a large church. Most of all, Sally has a deep, personal relationship with Christ that has sustained her and enabled her to rise above the stress of life.

It is our hope, not only that women will receive credible information, but also that they will be pointed to the strength available through a vital relationship with God. We pray that individual women's lives will be healed, marriages restored, churches strengthened, and, to some degree, society made more whole.

JIM CONWAY
Author, *Men in Mid-Life Crisis*

PART 1
YOUR HUSBAND'S MID-LIFE CRISIS

1
COMING UNGLUED

My husband angrily grabbed his coat and slammed out the door. My heart sank to my feet where it had been so often lately. But I thought we had been doing better recently. Yes, he still seemed depressed and confused much of the time, but generally he didn't blame me so much anymore.

As I watched Jim walk away down the snowy drive, I realized I had been off guard this evening. I had nagged a little bit here and there and had even questioned an insignificant decision he'd made. Until a few months ago he would have let these careless remarks go unchallenged. He was the one with the wide shoulders and the uncritical spirit. But then he had become hypersensitive, and I had to measure my words and reactions carefully. At times he would partially come out of his depression and be stronger emotionally, and then I would quickly forget to be careful.

I knew how much he hated the snow and cold, and since he wasn't adequately dressed, I didn't expect him to stay out long. Besides, this was the night before Thanksgiving and one of our daughters had arrived home from college only minutes before. We were planning a special welcome-back-home supper.

But Jim didn't return in time to eat with the family. We have a strong family tradition about waiting for everyone to gather before we eat, but each of the girls had other, previously arranged commitments, so they finally nibbled on something and went their ways. This kind of situation had never occurred before in our family. The special meal and I waited. I reset the table for two with special placemats and candles.

Eventually Jim did come back home. He accepted my apology and seemed amiable as we ate our meal together by candlelight. Little did I know how much was still raging within him—some anger toward me, but mostly confusion and terror from the deeper struggles he couldn't understand within himself. We went to bed, and he spent the night in a furious battle that I didn't know about until morning. I didn't know at the time how close I was to that being the last night we would have been together in our bed.[1]

IT SHOULDN'T HAPPEN TO HIM!

My husband is the senior pastor of a large church. He has faithfully preached and lived God's Word for over twenty-five years. Literally thousands of people have benefited from his wise counsel. God has given to him gifts of empathy, wisdom, insight, peacemaking, creativity—and the list could go on.

He is a thorough thinker and has learned to apply Scripture relevantly to daily living. His education has included two master's degrees and a doctorate from highly respected seminaries. His undergraduate work and his graduate programs have included much psychology as well as theology. With good foresight, he had as a young man set goals for his life that I frankly thought were beyond what he could ever attain. By his early forties he had met almost every one of those goals and had some additional fulfilling experiences besides.

We had three daughters who were growing in the Lord and were maturing into women of whom we were proud. We always had to be careful financially, but we lived in a nice house, thanks to our parents' help when we were young, and Jim's building and remodeling abilities. Our family had a great number of physical illnesses and injuries through the years, but we found these to be opportunities to grow and trust God. We were basically a happy and well-adjusted Christian family.

CRUMPLED LEADER

Then our strong leader with the optimistic outlook on life and nervy faith in the Lord began to quiver. He became depressed and grumpy. He began to doubt God's goodness and love. The messages he preached were still strong, but he told me privately that he felt like a hypocrite. He frequently had a compelling urge to run away. At first we thought he was simply overworked, so his desire to escape was natural. But the restlessness in him came from something deeper. He didn't understand much of it, but he did recognize it as the same phenomenon he had seen hit other men at this age.

He began to see the whole world in general, and our marriage in particular, as awful. He would declare, "Everything stinks!" Then it seemed as if he would try to bully me with philosophical questions such as, "Why did God make us in the first place? Why do we have to live this life?" He seemed obsessed with wanting to be young again and to enjoy those things he felt he had missed in his life of sacrifice. He often questioned the values by which he had lived. Of course, this was threatening to me since our lives were so entwined with each other.

YOURS TOO?

My husband's mid-life crisis has a happy ending. But perhaps your husband is just beginning the mid-life era. Or perhaps he's in the middle of his crisis and you're not sure there ever will be an end, let alone a happy one. Maybe you have noticed that other mid-life husbands were having problems but never thought it would happen to yours. Or perhaps you weren't even aware of a turmoil in other men in their middle years until you realized something was going wrong with your husband. However the awareness came to you, you now sense that your husband may be on the edge of disaster and you are scared—scared for him and scared for yourself.

The man you married, who has all the fine abilities and qualities, is changing. You may not have been telling him you appreciate him, but how can you when he is so hard to live with? You don't like his changes. Grouchiness and sharp words often replace his customary kindness and gentleness. Restlessness and vacillation erode his usual stable composure. Instead of exuding an air of confidence and boldness, he often seems anxious and insecure. Sometimes he wants to be babied; at other times he demands to be left alone. He is aloof and uncommunicating, or he lashes out irrationally at everyone and everything. He wears an air of martyrdom.

Formerly optimistic and challenged when difficulties came along, he now sits depressed and immobilized by self-pity. He sometimes lets obligations slip by without meeting them as he did faithfully for years. He finds excuses for not spending time with you or the children and shuns social activities at every opportunity. Perhaps he has resigned his leadership positions in the church, attends the services less frequently or not at all now, and sometimes voices profane complaints against God that greatly disturb you.

These changes in your mid-life husband are symptoms of a struggle going on inside him. He is battling with some very profound and basic, life-encompassing questions. Some of the outward manifestations of the questioning may be traumatic for you and for him, but the process is necessary. If your husband is around forty, his mid-life transition is taking him from the competitive, goal-centered, hard-driving days of his thirties into a more relaxed, more people-centered period. These may be anxious, confusing days for both of you, but if your husband successfully integrates the conflicts raging within him, there will be better days ahead. In fact, your marriage relationship will probably be more satisfying, his attitude toward his occupation or profession will improve, and he will be a better man in many ways.

WIN OR LOSE

As the wife of a husband who is experiencing a mid-life crisis, you need to know some basic facts. You can help him through this difficult time. Whether he blows it or grows through it can depend a great deal on your response. We're going to look at the problem from your husband's perspective and from yours. Then we're going

17

to examine what resources you have for yourself and what you can do to be of help to your husband at this difficult time.

But you have to decide if you're going to dig in and do the necessary work. Perhaps you've already been through so much with your husband that you are discouraged about trying. Or perhaps you don't believe there is such a thing as a mid-life crisis and you're not convinced you need to get involved. I'm convinced once you've considered the evidence for the existence of a mid-life crisis for men and learned how you can cope personally and how you can assist your husband, you'll want to work at a solution.

During Jim's crisis, however, I found that the determination to grit my teeth, bear the burden, turn the other cheek, and fill the air with positive thinking wasn't enough to carry me through the long, hard days—and nights. God's grace was also essential. I more than ever needed to have a good relationship with my Lord, who promised to be with me wherever I went and *whatever I went through.*

Right now you may want to take Isaiah 43:2-3 as your own special verses: "When you go through deep waters and great trouble, I will be with you. When you go through rivers of difficulty, you will not drown! (Wow! God, I'm glad you promised that because right about now the waters are closing over my head.) When you walk through the fire of oppression, you will not be burned up—the flames will not consume you. For I am the Lord your God, your Savior, . . ."

Now for the facts about the man's mid-life crisis.

2
THEY NEVER
WARNED ME!

A lot of time, effort, and money have been spent studying certain phases of life—childhood, adolescence, the senior years, and even women's menopause. But until recently there has been little acknowledgment that there are other stages in adult life. Thankfully, such people as Daniel Levinson,[1] Bernice Neugarten,[2] Alan Knox,[3] and Roger Gould[4] have been doing research in adult development in recent years. There is documented proof that adults do go through several transition times, and one of the most painful is at mid-life.

THE GAP

For years we have recognized that women experience varying degrees of stress at the time of menopause. In fact, most libraries have a number of volumes on the subject. But have you checked the shelves for books about men at mid-life? There are a few, but not many offer help or hope, and some border on the profane with lurid tales of the sexual escapades of mid-life men.

Many physicians, psychologists, and psychiatrists have been slow to admit that men go through a mid-life trauma. Perhaps it is because most of the professionals are men, and men must be strong, unswerving, and stable. That's the conditioning of our society. Perhaps medical doctors and counselors have been too busy with the urgent to reflect on the accumulated data of the symptoms of mid-life male patients and their wives. At least, the door is now beginning to open a little, and some doctors and therapists are acknowledging the results of research and their own observations.

NEW AWAKENING

Christians have also been silent on the subject. There wasn't much written about mid-life men from a Christian perspective until *Men in Mid-Life Crisis*[5] came along. If you've not read it, I suggest that you do, because it will tell you what a man goes through and give you a good background for what I'll be sharing here.

For a long time Christians thought that men in mid-life who began behaving in strange and sometimes un-Christlike ways had a spiritual defect or deliberately turned away from God. Their Christian brothers and sisters talked about them behind their backs so that they "could pray more intelligently for them." They were shunned and frequently confronted with "straighten up or get out of our fellowship!"

Some Christians are quick to grab the ammunition of 1 Corinthians 5 and the need for purity in the church, but they are slow to appropriate Galatians 6, which exhorts us to help a fellow Christian back onto the path (not kick him clear out of the garden!). That same verse also warns us to remember that we might be the next ones needing help. Some of us find it easier to stand upright and kick a fallen brother out of the way than to bend down—and maybe wrinkle our clothes and dirty our knees—to help him get up again. But our Lord commands us to share each other's troubles and problems. And the mid-life crisis *is* a problem! The Living Bible paraphrases Galatians 6: 3 in this way: "If anyone thinks he is too great to stoop to this, he is fooling himself. He is really a nobody."

The example of Jesus with the troubled and sinful, as seen in the Gospels, is one of understanding, kindness, and gentle guidance. The ones with whom he was harsh and direct were the rigid, follow-the-letter-of-the-law, religious people. Jesus took the time necessary to understand the problems and share the hurts of people. When Christians take the time to get into another's shoes, they are a lot less critical and a lot more understanding of the total situation.

MID-LIFE MOUNTAINS

More Christian counselors are now aware that men go through a real struggle during their mid-life transition. All that they have previously believed and worked hard for is under reappraisal. My husband has said, "It is a time when a man reaches the peak of a mountain range. He looks back over where he has come from and forward to what lies ahead. He also looks at himself and asks, 'Now that I've climbed the mountain, am I any different for it? Do I feel fulfilled? Have I achieved what I wanted to achieve?' "[6]

Jim also says, "How he evaluates his past accomplishment, hopes, and dreams will determine whether his life ahead will be an exhilarating challenge to him or simply a demoralizing distance that must be drearily traversed. In either case, he is at a time of trauma, because his emotions, as never before, are highly involved."[7]

Howard J. Clinebell, Jr., a Christian counselor and professor, in a discussion about understanding the midyears says,

> The changes and losses which accompany the movement from one life stage to another force us to learn new ways to satisfy our basic needs for self-esteem, meaning, identity,. and nurturing relationships. . . . [This] normally brings feelings of grief, pressure, and anxiety. For some persons the entrance into [the] mid-years . . . produces obvious crises with acute anxiety and floundering behavior. . . . [For others the transition] produces a quiet crisis which is painful though not devastating.[8]

Jim and I have learned from talking to hundreds of men and women that many men everywhere are experiencing a traumatic time at mid-life. The stories they and their wives tell are often heart shredding and nearly all fall into a predictable pattern:

"John was a kind, loving husband and father who spent time with our family. He was a spiritual leader in our church. He was working overtime at his job to provide for us. Some time ago he began behaving strangely. He became irritable and depressed. He spent money we didn't have to buy different clothes and a sports car (or a motorcycle). He seems obsessed with trying to look young. He insisted on taking a vacation without me. Now I've learned that he is seeing another woman (or he has entirely left home to be alone, or he is living with another woman). He claims our marriage hasn't been any good for years, and it's all my fault. He has become cross and unreasonable with our children and says we are all just parasites living off him."

THE TIP OF THE ICEBERG

Some research shows that as much as eighty percent of American men suffer moderate to severe symptoms in making the mid-life transition,[9] while other studies show the figure to be almost one-hundred percent.[10] By the year 2000 the largest U. S. population group will shift from youth to mid-life. The number of adults between thirty-five and forty-five will increase by seventy-five percent while the numbers of youth will increase by five percent.[11] These numbers mean that a larger number of mid-life men and their wives will be undergoing a similar stress at the same time. We'd better understand the phenomenon, prepare for it, and do some things to help make positive outcomes for ourselves and the coming generation.

Because of the secrecy and ignorance surrounding many of the real concerns of mid-life men, each man and his family have often suffered alone. They have felt that the internal struggles and external events were peculiar to them, not realizing they were part of a normal developmental pattern. Tangible research evidence that the mid-life crisis is a common occurrence is mounting and the word needs to get out.

WHEN DOES IT HIT?

Daniel Levinson and his team at Yale University recently spent ten years (1967-1977) studying forty men in detail. Their findings have led Dr. Levinson to say, "At around 40 a crucial developmental change occurs. . . . The Mid-Life Transition ordinarily has its onset at age 40 or 41 and

23

lasts about five years. For the fifteen men in our sample who completed this period, the average age at termination was 45.5, the range 44 to 47."[12]

Your husband or someone you know who is showing the symptoms of such a crisis may be older or younger than those men in the Levinson study when he started his mid-life questioning. Perhaps he neglected to recognize or confront the mid-life issues when they were first presented to him. Our own work with mid-life people as well as other research indicates that the mid-life crisis range may be wider, occurring as early as thirty-five for some men and as late as fifty-five for others. Sometimes an external event, such as loss of a parent or friend or a drastic change in job status, forces a man into an open battle with the internal evaluation that is going on. Sometimes, however, a tragedy causes him to suppress the questions until later.

THE URGENCY OF "NOW"

Roger Gould, who has a private practice in psychiatry and is a researcher at the University of California at Los Angeles, has for several years gathered evidence about adult development from sixteen to fifty and concluded that in mid-life "we see more clearly, and consequently we are more frightened." He continues, "For we know that we *must* act on our new vision of ourselves and the world. The desire for stability and continuity which characterized our thirties is being replaced by a relentless inner demand for action. The sense of timelessness in our early thirties is giving way to an awareness of the pressure of time in our forties. *Whatever we must do must be done now!*"[13]

Another problem for many mid-life men is that they don't know who they are. A man may have lived all these years not assessing who he is as a person and not exercising his individuality. Dr. James Kilgore says:

> They are molded by mothers, teachers, wives, vocational expectations, company policy and so on until they literally do not know who they are. The result for many men is the seed of later rebellion. Edmund Bergler called it "the revolt of the middle-aged man." When a man finally feels he has given the basics to his wife and children, he often reacts rashly, reaching out for what he may have missed—clothes, a new car, time off for recreation. These symbols of his rebellion are but the outward responses to an inner frustration which has been present for some time—a sense of depersonalization.[14]

During twenty years of pastoral counseling, my husband, Jim, began to recognize the mid-life stress as a common phenomenon. Wives usually were the first ones who came to him about marriage problems, but occasionally the men also came for help. He eventually noticed that the behaviors and stresses of the men around forty fell into a similar pattern. Then Jim experienced his own mid-life crisis! During this time we were both doing research to write *Men in Mid-Life Crisis*. After some agonizing months, Jim reached a climax in his experience and the Lord gave him some assurances that he was indeed going to make it with his life still intact. The manuscript for the book was finished and Jim was able to offer some tried and true helps.

"THAT'S MY HUSBAND!"

As soon as the book began to be circulated, we were further convinced that the male mid-life crisis was indeed a fact and that it was rampant all over the United States. Telephone calls and letters came from hundreds of women telling us the book had described their husbands to a T! When we spoke on the subject over radio or television or at conferences, responses from men and women, believers and unbelievers, overwhelmingly showed that they identified with the crisis.

Jim developed a multimedia production to further illustrate the mid-life situation when he spoke at meetings. He took scores of pictures of mid-life men on beaches, in physical fitness centers, in sports car salesrooms, in offices, at construction sites, and other places. Each time he asked permission to take the pictures, he would explain why he wanted them. As he described the mid-life crisis to these men, everyone of them acknowledged that he was in the midst of such a trial right then. Many were surprised and relieved to know that other men also experienced the problem.

Convinced that there really is some amount of upheaval at mid-life, we need to ask why it is so often traumatic or, at best, unsettling.

3
WHY SO MUCH
AT ONE TIME?

Can't the mid-life time be one of quiet evaluation—appraising the past and setting new sights for the future—and getting on with living? Why must men go through so much introspection and weird behavior? Wives of husbands who have been generally stable, dependable, and optimistic are especially bewildered. Some new thing has hit their husbands and they are afraid the change is permanent.

Dr. Levinson notes that because mid-life men are often somewhat irrational, others may regard them as "upset" or "sick," but what they are going through is normal. (That doesn't mean it isn't painful, but it *is* normal.) He "is working on normal mid-life tasks," according to Levinson, and "the desire to question and modify his life stems from the most healthy part of the self."[1]

At first I found it hard to understand why Jim needed to analyze every aspect of his life when he was in his midforties. I didn't always realize all that he was evaluating, but when he let me know, it seemed strange to me that he couldn't simply accept life as it was. As he shared more about his struggles with aging and the meaning of life, I could begin to see that he had to think through a whole lot of things. And often he wanted to be alone to do it.

A "MOLDY OLDY"

A man near forty has reached the time in life when he—and others—can notice the physical changes taking place in his body, he has often experienced the zenith of success in his occupation, and he is acutely aware that he is now on a different generation level. He can do some things to keep his body in shape and to improve his physical appearance and endurance, but he cannot actually stop the aging process. He cannot deny a gradual decline in certain physical aspects—hair color or loss, eyesight, reflexes, muscle tone, weight shift—that signal, as someone has aptly said, "life's slow but certain slide downhill."[2]

By forty he realizes that he has either gone as far as he will go in his occupation or he doesn't have much time left to do it. If he is not pleased with his attainments, he is facing the fact that he may never succeed as he had dreamed. If he has met all his goals, he has learned that he still isn't satisfied. A man's self-worth is greatly tied to his work and his ability to keep pushing and creating. Our culture values youth and production, so his wisdom, insight, and more mellow approach to his profession may not be appreciated. He can be replaced, and that is frightening to his self-esteem and for his financial future.

Prior to forty he was considered a part of the younger generation in the life cycle, but he must now acknowledge that he is considered to be in an older generation. People in their twenties do not regard him as a peer but, in Levinson's words, as " 'dad' rather than 'buddy.' "[3] His role with his aging parents is probably reversing, and he is now becoming their nurturer. He may need to assist them financially, but most likely he needs to help them in emotional ways by spending more time with them and guiding them in the decisions they face. He begins to acknowledge that in too short a time *he* will be the senior citizen needing nurturing from his children.

Betty shared with me how her pastor-husband, Ralph, had thought he'd finally have it made when he got old enough to be respected for his wisdom and experience. By the time he was in his forties he was senior pastor in a church with three younger staff members. Ralph envisioned them all working together as a team, but two of them were immature and he had to hover over them to see that their share of the ministry got done. The third was very independent and had no desire to blend his work with the others. In fact, he began to work behind Ralph's back to gather a portion of the congregation around himself and eventually tried to oust Ralph.

This all happened at a time when Ralph's father was dying of cancer and their last child had gone away to college. Betty could see that Ralph was grieving more over the absence of their son than over the impending loss of his father. In fact, he sometimes resented his father's need for attention while he was so consumed with trying to hold the church together and to keep his position. Betty felt very anxious about the church situation and she too missed their son, but she wisely realized her husband was suffering even more than she was. Betty took time to let him talk about his problems and fears, and he was eventually strong enough to work with his circumstances.

LIFE WITH HIS WIFE

A man's marriage may be the biggest source of unrest. While he was busy succeeding in his career and his wife was busy with hers or with raising the children, their own relationship may not have been growing. Now when he is questioning the deeper meaning of all the things he has been doing and deciding if he wants to continue in the same routine, his marriage may seem unsatisfying and downright miserable. Affairs, divorces, and remarriages are common during mid-life as some men decide the commitments they made in their early twenties are no longer valid or satisfying.

Irritants and disagreements that existed in the relationship all along but were ignored now become festering sores. Because a man often doesn't understand the reason for his restlessness and depression, he finds it easy to blame his wife. He begins to feel that the marriage has always been poor and they probably made a mistake to marry in the first place. He exaggerates the negatives in his marriage because he tends at this time to see all of life in a poor light.

Most often his wife is unprepared for this blame and rejection, and, besides, she has a list of complaints of her own. Since she doesn't understand the transition through which her husband is going, she doesn't know it is only temporary. She often aggravates the situation with her own poor reactions and decisions. Yes, it's natural and understandable for her to behave badly, but it only worsens the dilemma.

One day we received an agonizing phone call from Carol after her husband, Gary, had left her. Through her tears she explained that they had been having stormy times the last few months. Gary had become unusually restless and cross with her and the children. Then he had started coming home late from work. When she demanded explanations, he got angry. She was afraid he was being unfaithful to her. Finally one night she accused him of being late because he was seeing another woman. He retorted that if he was, it wasn't any of her business. She felt it was and kept after him to tell her one way or the other. He refused to answer and went off to watch tv. This confirmed her suspicions. Alone in the bedroom she cried and prayed and wrung her hands.

Finally she decided to have it out with him. She charged into the family room, punched off the tv, and demanded that they have an honest talk. Gary ordered her to turn the tv back on and leave him alone as he had nothing to say to her. Carol lost her temper and began to scream at him about taking time for everything else but her. He became furious, slammed out of the house, and was gone until very late.

Several more such episodes occurred, sometimes over her suspicions of another woman and sometimes because he wasn't taking care of things around the house any more or he was threatening to sell his business. Finally during a fight one night, he left and hadn't returned. Carol was convinced he had become impossible and their marriage was over, so she filed for a divorce which was to be finalized in a month. Then she had read *Men in Mid-Life Crisis* and had begun to understand her husband a little and realized she had handled things improperly. What could she do now?

TOPSY-TURVY

To a man in his forties, his life is like a pile of important papers someone has tossed into the air that the breeze from a nearby fan tosses and tumbles even more. As they fall and scatter on the floor and under the furniture, he has to bend down and gather them up. As he does, he realizes he is tired, dizzy, and discouraged. He has to sort and reorganize the papers and decide if some should be discarded or rewritten. And it certainly would help if his wife and the boss weren't standing there, nagging and pressuring him while he tries to put the pieces back together!

I like the way Dr. Levinson describes the situation:

> Every aspect of their lives comes into question. . . . A profound reappraisal of this kind cannot be a cool, intellectual process. It must involve emotional turmoil, despair, the sense of not knowing where to turn or of being stagnant and unable to move at all. A man in this state often makes false starts. He tentatively tests a variety of new choices, not only out of confusion or impulsiveness but, equally, out of a need to explore, to see what is possible, to find out how it feels to engage in a particular love relationship, occupation or solitary pursuit. *Every genuine reappraisal must be agonizing, because it challenges the illusions and vested interests on which the existing structure is based.* [4]

When a man has to evaluate the existing structures of his life and decide which parts to keep or modify and which to discard, he experiences so much turmoil that it often shows in his behavior.

CHRISTIANS ARE SUSCEPTIBLE, TOO

"But if he is a committed Christian, won't he avoid all that?" many ask. My husband's reply is, "That's like telling a ten-year-old that he can avoid the adolescent years by becoming a Christian!"

We recognize that adolescence is a normal developmental stage. Every teenager has certain emotional tasks to be accomplished in order to become a healthy, mature adult. Psychologists and sociologists are now recognizing the mid-life transition as a normal stage of development. Have you noticed how similar the symptoms of mid-life and adolescence are? That's because the people involved have similar evaluation processes to complete. The major differences are that mid-life men carry a lot more responsibilities, have more people depending on them, and are beginning to experience decreasing physical vigor and society's disrespect for age.

If a teenager is a Christian who appropriates God's resources, he will certainly go through his years of testing and deciding his life's values more easily. But that doesn't keep him from having to go through adolescence. Likewise, being a committed Christian is a decided advantage for the mid-life man, but it doesn't prevent him from experiencing a transition time and working through the necessary tasks of this stage of life.

EXCESS BAGGAGE

How smoothly the transition is made depends upon many factors, such as what kind of emotional baggage he has carried over from earlier years, whether he made a wise occupation choice in the beginning that was in line with his talents and abilities, and whether his marriage is satisfying and growing. Feigenbaum, who has conducted studies with upper-middle-class men, found that the severity of a man's mid-life crisis was also influenced by birth order (the firstborn shows more severe symptoms), the wife's perception of the problem, and whether or not the man is in a power struggle with his children.[5] There are some experts who feel that a mid-life man's struggle may be less severe if he has thoroughly worked through adolescent and young adult issues of autonomy, inter-dependence, intimacy, and identity.

Dave was forty-one when he went into severe depression and rebellion. He and Anita had been married twenty-one years. They were both young when they were married, after Dave's second year of college. He had been living with his parents until then. He was the older of two sons and had stayed at home to save money while going to college and to help out with the family's small business. His younger brother had gone to a college farther away.

During his third year of school and first year of marriage, Dave dropped out of college to work because Anita was expecting and had to quit her job. Dave intended to go back to school as soon as they got on their feet financially, but babies and medical bills continued to come. He finally gave up the hope of getting a college degree and continued to work in the insurance office where he originally thought he'd be only temporarily. He received promotions through the years and the pay was good, but he had planned to be a civil engineer and never felt content in the insurance business.

In her late thirties Anita decided to go back to work. She also decided to take night classes at the junior college so she would be eligible for a better position with her company. Their four children were still at home and often were left on their own. Two of them began having trouble in school and the oldest started hanging around with a tough bunch of kids.

Dave decided it was time to crack down, but he didn't get far. His teenagers were belligerent and disrespectful. Anita was gone much of the time and tired when she was home. He began to resent her freedom and her lack of interest in him. He also felt it was time for his brother to help care for their elderly parents, but the burden still

34

fell mostly on him.

After two or three years of hassling with his children, heavy responsibilities for his parents, and disinterest on the part of his wife, Dave was coming apart when he called my husband. Jim worked with him for several months before he began to heal and to resolve some of his intense struggles.

We have begun to understand a little bit about a man's mid-life crisis, but what about a woman's crisis? She has some distinctive problems of her own.

4

BUT WHO CARES
ABOUT ME?

Women go through a series of developmental stages, too, and woe be it if you are going through your mid-life crisis when your husband is going through his! If you are not, you are in a better position to minister to him. And, hopefully, when you have your special adjustment times, he will be strong enough to help you through yours.

BALANCING THE SYSTEM

William Lederer and Dr. Don Jackson in *The Mirages of Marriage* support a premise Jim and I have found to be true in our marriage. A marriage works on a "systems" concept. The whole is *more* than the sum of its parts. The whole is made up of all the parts *plus* the manner in which the parts operate in relation to one another.

Lederer and Jackson point out:

According to the systems concept, a change occurs when related parts are rearranged—be they atoms or the behavior of closely associated human beings, such as two people who are married. . . .
The systems concept postulates that there is a constant action-reaction between associated things. The closer the association, the more obvious is the action-reaction. If an influence upsets the balance between the associated entities, then a compensating factor is provided *by the system* to regain balance. . . .
Marriage is not just a rigid relationship between two rigid individuals. Marriage is a fluid relationship between two spouses and their two individual systems of behavior. The totality of marriage is determined by how the spouses operate (behave) in relation to each other. . . . In physics it is accepted that for every action there is an equal reaction. The same law holds in psychology—in human relationships.[1]

A balance has to be maintained in a marriage relationship. If you are sick and need care, your husband's response has to be one of nurturing and helping to fill the gap that your illness has created. If he is not well in some way himself, you may have to find extra strength in yourself that you may not have noticed before. Jim has found in his counseling experience that many mid-life women possess a great deal of strength and endurance in coping with the situations created by their husband's mid-life crisis that they never thought they had.[2]

MID-THIRTIES TRAUMA

Some of a mid-life woman's strength may come from the fact that she has recently weathered her own reevaluation time. Psychologists and sociologists are recognizing that most women experience an unsettling time in the last half of their thirties.[3] Age is catching up with them, usually a little sooner than for their husbands. Their children are off to school all day and need them less. If they chose a career outside the home, it is becoming routine or they are being threatened by younger, sharper women, and they wonder if they should have invested life this way. And their husbands are often so engrossed in the demands of their careers that they have little time for them.

They begin to question their worth, their choices, and their values. Gail Sheehy calls it "the crossroads for women."[4] Some decide that now is their last chance to make life different. Thirty-five is the most common age of the runaway wife. There is now one runaway wife for every two runaway husbands, compared to one in three hundred in 1974.[5]

MENOPAUSAL MISERIES

There is also the long-acknowledged menopausal stage for women. This generally begins near the end of the forties or beginning of the fifties. Hopefully, your husband will by that time be safely through his mid-life crisis and will have developed into that more mellow, sensitive, loving person that studies predict he will.

Some women go through their climacteric years with little difficulty. Others suffer a great deal physically and emotionally. Some physicians say a woman's emotional troubles during this time come from how she handles external circumstances and preexisting problems and are not caused by menopause itself. Other medical doctors and counselors, however, feel that nutrition and hormonal balance affect emotional stability during this time and a woman cannot simply "will" herself to be strong.

Both the late-thirties evaluation time and the climacteric years are crucial times in women's lives. Jim and I are now doing the research for an entire book on these themes, since they merit a lengthier consideration.

Now let's go into detail on the wife's problems while her husband is in *his* mid-life crisis.

PART 2
YOUR DILEMMA

5
LIFE OF A MID-LIFE WIFE

A husband's mid-life crisis is going to cause a wife some of the greatest stresses that she has ever experienced. She will be shocked to see her husband begin to question values and choices she thought had been settled long ago. She will have trouble understanding why he is so taken up with his aging. When he accuses her of being the cause of his problems or gives her the cold, silent treatment, she will feel rejected and misunderstood.

The reality of her husband being attracted to younger women will cause her terrible anxiety, because she knows she doesn't have the figure she once had, even if she has been careful about diet and exercise. But, after all, she bore his children, sat up nights with them, now chauffeurs them, administers their comings and goings, and has been doing double duty with them and the house, and perhaps a job besides, for all these years. Of course, she has crow's-feet at the corners of her eyes and her hair is graying! She wishes he could accept her aging—and his.

If he is having trouble at work or has perhaps even quit, there will be financial strain. His self-esteem has probably taken a beating, so he will take out his frustrations on his wife and kids. Because he is grouchy and irritable, his wife will have to cover for him with family and friends. She will make excuses when he withdraws and refuses to be involved. If she babies him, he will want her to leave him alone; if she ignores him, he will want her attention.

In such a situation a wife will find herself on the horns of a dilemma. She may try to help her husband see the world straight, but he seems to be wearing the wrong glasses, and they certainly aren't rose-colored either! She may feel as if she is tiptoeing over rotten eggs all the time. One misstep and phew-yyy!!

WHO ARE YOU?

If you allow yourself to think about life without your husband, you will probably be scared at first. Your life revolves around him and the kids. You will wonder how the family would manage financially. The kids' lives would be ripped apart without him, and that would intensify your misery. You're back to where you started in your mulling over your present situation. Life with him is sheer agony, but without him it would be worse.

Several recently published women's books blast the present mid-life woman for having settled for finding her identity only in being the wife of her husband and the mother of her children. As she reaches this time in life, her children hardly need her and her husband may be dissatisfied with her or take her for granted. Therefore, they say, she loses all she has lived for. This may be true to a certain extent, but can it not be equally as tragic for a woman to be thoroughly involved in a career outside the home and find that to be her only identity? If it is wrong to be only Mrs. John Jones or the mother of Bobby Jones, is it not as sad to be only personnel manager, television producer, or vice-president in charge of production? I have had careers both in my home and outside, and I don't find the outside one to be any more satisfying and certainly not as rewarding as the inside one.

Your identity needs to be drawn from the quality of person you are, wherever you are. True, you are known by what you do, but you should be known by your *being* while you are *doing*. You need to be flexible and realize that your roles may change, whether you are a wife, mother, or employee, but you are still the same person and you have a mission in life.

A woman with Christ in control of every aspect of her life has an advantage. She has an identity in Him. (See 1 John 3:1-2 and Eph. 1:6.) She also has God's Word and His Spirit within her to cause her to mature. (See such exciting verses as 2 Peter 1:3-4; Gal. 5:22, and Phil. 1:6.) The capstone verse for me is, ". . . we Christians actually do have within us a portion of the very thoughts and mind of Christ" (1 Cor. 2:16b). That ought to make a difference!

Let's face it, though, your husband's mid-life crisis will make you reevaluate your identity. What he decides to do with his life affects yours. Are you still you if he changes jobs or quits work entirely? Who are you if he has an affair or divorces you?

FEELING SHREDDED

Tied closely to your identity is your emotional life. Actually, all your parts are closely knit—emotions, spiritual life, physical being, social person, and so on—and cannot be divided into isolated segments. Each affects the others. Your emotions, however, probably get batted around the hardest of all during your husband's trauma.

Jim and I asked women across the United States to respond to a questionnaire about life during their husbands' mid-life crisis. Following are some of the emotions women felt as a result of how their husbands were behaving:

Insecure
Anxious
Rejected
Confused
Afraid
Scared to be alone at night
Hateful
Jealous
Worthless
Angry at God
Unloved
Lonely
Naggy and pushy
Withdrawn
Desirous of escape

You could probably add some more. I found that some of the emotions I felt couldn't be identified, but I experienced very definite physical symptoms from them. It was like being wrung through a wringer and then run over by the sharp wheels of a heavy freight train. It was like icy water piercing through the membranes of my stomach. One minute I could be hopeful; the next minute I was back to feeling anxious and afraid. Each new development brought another set of feelings to deal with.

ON OR OFF WITH GOD

In the questionaire we asked women about their spiritual lives during the crisis. Some drew closer to the Lord and learned from him; others felt more distant and angry at him. Some continued attending church services and Bible studies; others quit because of embarrassment over their situation or because of the way other church members treated them. Some spent a lot of time in prayer; others couldn't pray. Some said they learned to genuinely accept Christ's forgiveness and help. Others felt they became less judgmental of others.

Those who turned to the Lord with their problem felt he had been faithful in strengthening them and helping them improve in needed areas, even though their prayers for their husbands may not have been answered in the manner they wanted or as soon as they hoped. Those who studied their Bibles and claimed its promises felt that the struggle had been worth it because of the spiritual maturity and closer fellowship with the Lord that they experienced.

MISFITTING INTO SOCIETY

A husband's mid-life crisis cannot help but affect his wife's life with other people. She must often cover up for him and make excuses for his behavior. She may find herself dodging certain topics of conversation or hedging on her answers to friends' and relatives' questions. Some women learn they have no true friends at this time, and they are very lonely. Other women, however, find that their friends are the kind who support and encourage them.

Often a woman either has to stay home or go alone to social functions. If she goes alone, she is considered the

YOUR DILEMMA

"odd duck" in the group. If her husband has actually left her, she feels stranger than ever in social situations and is sometimes left out altogether. If she is divorced, she becomes a threat to other women who don't want her around their husbands, and some men think she is now fair game for their advances.

MISUSED AND ABUSED

Physically, a wife suffers, too. The tension makes her tired. Sometimes the fatigue is so great she would drop under ordinary circumstances, but she feels she must keep going so things don't get worse. She often doesn't get enough sleep because of worry, waiting for her husband to come home, or a long argument late at night. She may overeat or not eat enough of the right foods. Ulcers, acne, menstrual complications, headaches, heart trouble, and other symptoms come from the stress her body is under.

Some women are physically abused by their husbands during this time. In their anger and frustration with the unsettled issues within themselves, some previously gentle men have become violent and have beaten or otherwise harmed their wives. In fact, wife beating is becoming a serious national problem. Because women are trying to shield their husbands or protect their reputations, or because they feel they deserve it, they often do not report the beating or get help for themselves.

SEXUAL STRESS

A wife's sexual life is probably altered during this time, too. Many men experience impotence at this age, though most cases prove to be psychological rather than physical. There is a natural decline in male sexual ability by mid-life, but if accepted as normal the change can be sexually positive rather than negative. His speed at reaching orgasm may be slower and the frequency of his orgasms may be less, but his effectiveness as a satisfying lover to his wife can be greater. A man may be threatened by the fact that his wife is becoming more sexually aggressive and emancipated, a documented phenomenon for women at this age.[1]

Sarah and Frank had experienced a strange turn of events in their sex life as they neared their twenty-fifth anniversary. Sarah began to attempt to initiate sexual encounters, something she had never done before. She bought seductive nightgowns and tried various other enticements. Instead of responding positively, Frank was cold and disinterested. Sometimes his withdrawn attitude dampened Sarah's spirits so that she went to sleep frustrated. A few times her enthusiasm and sexual advances won out, but more often Frank complained that he just didn't "have it" anymore.

Even if a husband's sexual functioning and desires are nearly the same as in precrisis days, a wife's tensions over other aspects of his behavior may inhibit her emotions for a satisfying sexual relationship. If her husband is having an affair, his sexual ability with her may be limited. And you can believe that if he is having an affair and she knows it, *her* sexual ability with him will be altered!

THE FINANCIAL CRUNCH

When we asked women how their financial situation was during their husband's crisis, many replied that it was difficult, especially if the husband had left the home and was paying for housing elsewhere for himself. Sometimes finances are drained if the husband indulges in his desire for a sports car or another expensive item he has previously denied himself. Some men, according to the answers on the questionnaires, were still providing as usual for their families, a few were even more generous, and some others were doing less because they were spending more money on themselves or friends, or due to a job change. Some families lost benefits such as health and life insurance if the husband had quit his job. Under some company policies, divorcees lost all benefits. One woman reported that housing and money were less important now that she was more concerned about bettering the relationship with her husband.

We have thought a little about some of the things that happen to a mid-life woman personally during her husband's crisis. What about her marriage relationship itself?

6
LIFE WITH A MID-LIFE MAN

Even though a woman and her husband may have had a fairly stable marriage, the mid-life crisis will surely test it. If there have been unresolved problems before the crisis, they will be magnified. A poor marriage will get even worse and may not, in fact, stand the strain.

Bill and Helen are a typical example. When they married twenty years ago, Bill was still quite emotionally immature. Helen was very strong-minded and began to do most of the decision making for the family. Bill didn't notice, because he usually didn't even recognize that decisions needed to be made. Helen also had definite opinions about how Bill should do things, including his work, and she was always sure to pass on her insights to him. She did so in the form of criticism, ridicule, and nagging.

Eventually Bill came to resent her domineering ways, but he did not have the courage to confront her about it. As her bossiness became more oppressive to him, he escaped by taking a job that required a lot of travel and nights away from home. Because of the amount of time they spent away from each other, they grew apart in their interests and in keeping up with each other's daily happenings. Helen had to manage the family while Bill was away, so she continued running things even when he was home for a day or a weekend.

As Bill entered his forties, he began to realize that life was slipping by, his children were growing up and ready to leave home, and he didn't know them or his wife anymore. He began to long for intimacy with his family. Yet, when he would spend more time at home, Helen made him feel he no longer belonged and she picked at him incessantly. He didn't like being on the road, but he couldn't stand being at home.

THE ONLY WAY IS OUT

Bill and Helen finally sought a counselor when Bill told Helen he wanted a divorce. Helen was shocked because she felt they had a good marriage. When the counselor talked to them together, he noticed that Helen dominated the session. When the counselor asked her if she understood some of her husband's needs, she quickly and strongly said, "Of course." The counselor noticed Bill wince. It soon became apparent that Helen knew little about Bill's needs, his personality, his views, his values, or any aspect of his life—and she was unaware of her ignorance. Bill did not know how to express himself to her or confront her about her domineering ways. His solution was to try to escape.

With the counselor's help they each began to see their

own part in the situation. They decided they were willing to work on the problems. As Helen backed off with her bossiness and Bill began to communicate his thoughts and feelings, their relationship improved rapidly. They started taking time to understand each other and to work at meeting each other's needs. Soon they found they had fallen in love again. Of course, they still had to keep working at their weak spots, because people do not instantaneously break poor life-style patterns that have been followed for years. However, they were both Christians and relied on God's power to help them change. Now that they had tasted the joy of a better marriage, they had the necessary motivation to keep working at it.

LOW TIDE

Marriage by mid-life years is usually at its lowest ebb in satisfaction. Gould reports this to be true from his studies of married couples.[1] A young couple start married life feeling close, spending time together, doing things to please each other, enjoying their sexual experiences, and expecting continued bliss. As they each get busy with their own careers and the children, it is harder to find time to communicate adequately and to keep up with each other's daily lives. Answering the demands of other urgent matters robs them of the intimacy that keeps them in touch with each other. The less they know each other, the easier it is to drift still farther apart.

When the mid-life crisis hits a man, he needs the help a strong marriage can give, and he is least likely to have it now than at any other time. His wife doesn't realize or may not care that he is struggling. He finds it hard to let her know. Their communication is only about the business of running the family. They no longer exchange ideas or talk about their feelings. Their sexual relationship may be almost nonexistent because they are always tired and busy. They find their married life dull, boring, and, if there is strife between them, miserable.

THE BALL AND CHAIN

Because a husband at this age often feels trapped by his responsibilities and wants to escape from them, he finds it easy to blame his wife for his predicament. He is tired of having to work hard to keep up with the heavy expenses and everyone's demands on him for his time, energy, and decisions. Since his emotions aren't as stable as they were previously, he is apt to look back over the years of his marriage and remember only the bad times. Because he is weighing his value structure, he is probably questioning whether choices and commitments he made fifteen or twenty-five years ago are going to fit him in his future. The conclusion might cause him to consider changing his marital commitment.

"Besides," he thinks, "this woman is getting old and she reminds me that I am getting old, too. I feel a lot better around younger women." Women, my husband said to warn you that you are in competition! It isn't a fair competition, but you *are* competing. You are being judged according to your youth—youthful figure, youthful face, youthful playfulness, youthful interests, youthful vigor. There's no way that you can win under those standards. You have to compete and win in other ways. We will talk about how to be a more attractive person later.

Because you are busy with your own concerns, you may resent the time it takes for your husband's crisis. Your communication may be so poor that you have no idea what he is going through, and you don't want to bother to find out. Or you may feel he can be ordered to "snap out of it" and the rest is up to him.

Perhaps he has never been the leader he should be, and you've *had* to take over. Now he is complaining that you are too bossy. Or he may have led in the past, but now he says he can't. Sometimes he wants you to make decisions. Other times he resents it if you do.

NOW WHERE?

The whole course of your marriage relationship for the present and the future seems uncharted, and the maps you've been following seem to be faulty. You may feel like a little girl lost on an unfamiliar path in the woods at night. What do you do now? The roles you have each been living out are now in need of reevaluation. Your family situation has changed, and so have you.

Surely there must be some absolutes to follow.

There are. And now is the time to do some careful searching of God's Word about husband-and-wife relationships. You also need to do some thoughtful study of your personalities, your history together, your life-style, and your total family experience as you think about God's absolutes. Sometimes we quickly decide on pat guidelines and force our mates and our children to follow them whether or not they are really the right guidelines for our particular family.

God gets the credit (or blame) for a lot of neat one-two-three steps to right relationships that really are man-made (or *woman*-made) or have come down from a long line of tradition that had its beginnings in pagan culture. For instance, a lot of the view of husband-and-wife roles in marriage today comes from ancient Jewish tradition that was influenced, not by God's commands and principles, but by the surrounding pagan world. Husband-and-wife roles continue to be distorted by those who promote the dominant male-subordinate female theory or those who advocate female manipulation of men. One extreme is as bad as the other. An unbiased look at the meaning of the original language of the Bible on these subjects is an eye-opener.[2]

During this transition time for you and your husband, you can do some careful weighing of Scripture, study good Christian books, and ponder the counsel of godly people in deciding God's way of living out the nitty-gritty details of your marriage. The information from these good sources might be conflicting and still leave you baffled, but God promises to give you wisdom, if you ask for it. I've found that if I quit fretting about what to do in a particular situation, quiet down a minute, and ask God for his wisdom, he really does give it! ". . . he is always ready to give a bountiful supply of wisdom to all who ask him. . . ." (James 1: 5).

WEIGHING THE WAY

How can I tell if the thoughts that come to me are God's wisdom and not my own thoughts, imaginations, and desires? James 3: 17 gives us some tests to determine if the wisdom is from the Lord. Any insight I claim or course of action I feel led to take must line up with these criteria. "But the wisdom that comes from heaven is first of all pure and full of quiet gentleness. Then it is peace-loving and courteous. It allows discussion and is willing to yield to others; it is full of mercy and good deeds. It is wholehearted and straightforward and sincere."

God's wisdom is pure—undefiled by my selfishness, past grievances, suspicions, or unrealistic hopes that my husband is going to do what I want him to do. True wisdom is quietly gentle, loves peace, and is considerate. A lot of so-called insight from the Lord would fail right at this very point of being courteous. Spiritual wisdom has room for discussion and hearing the other point of view. It is even willing to yield to the other one! Godly wisdom is compassionate and then follows up this understanding of another's plight with action ("good deeds") to alleviate the problems.

SINCERELY WRONG

God's wisdom is enthusiastically candid ("wholehearted and straightforward"). Perhaps the ability to be outspoken on a subject is the one criterion of wisdom that is easiest for us to use—and misuse. We often misinterpret boldness alone as the sure sign of wisdom when, in fact, being outspoken must be carefully balanced with all the other facets of wisdom.

True wisdom is also sincere. Sincerity by itself cannot be a test of wisdom, because we can be sincerely wrong. That's why we need the balance of courtesy and listening to the other's point of view.

It is easy to make some bold and sincere decisions that we mistake as being God's leading when we consider only our side of a situation. Allowing discussion and being willing to yield to others, however, is more apt to ensure God's wisdom in my decisions. True spiritual wisdom can stand the strain of listening to another's side. If I am too threatened to hear another point of view, then I need to be aware of the sources of my wisdom.

Allowing for discussion means that you and your husband need to be communicating well. Busyness and carelessness may cause each of you not to really know the other's thoughts and feelings well enough to understand the other one's needs or to meet those needs. You may have lost a great deal of emotional intimacy and may not even realize it.

HIS NEED FOR INTIMACY

Because intimacy is gone and not missed doesn't mean it isn't needed. At any given time in life, an individual has a certain set of needs, whether or not he acknowledges them. He either consciously or unconsciously does what is necessary to meet those needs. A man may need someone to listen to him, to help him think through the things he is wrestling with, to encourage him to go through his reevaluation process. If he and his wife are not communicating well with each other, she may not recognize his need and he may think she doesn't care or wouldn't understand.

There may be another woman available, however, who does seem to understand and care. If a man begins to spend time sharing with her, he may find himself involved in an affair that he never intended to take place. Previously he might have avoided becoming entangled with another woman, but at mid-life he is very vulnerable because of the confusion, frustration, and dissatisfaction he is experiencing about every aspect of his life. The forces that come to bear upon him at this time of life push him into a corner he's never been in before.

The situation may be complicated by his blaming his wife for all his problems. Perhaps he feels she is the cause of his entrapment in work responsibilities he no longer wants to face, she doesn't care about him as a person, or she is nothing but a nagging mother to him. Right or wrong, he may make any number of accusations against her. Probably he will not let her even know much of what he feels. Neither is he aware of all he is feeling, but he may feel justified in pulling away from his wife because, in his perception, she is the cause of his unhappiness.

How does a wife handle the situation if her husband becomes involved in an affair?

7
LIFE IN A TRIANGLE

Generally, a mid-life man does not deliberately set out to find someone with whom he can have an affair. The other woman is most often a person he already knows and with whom he has natural contact in the routine of life. She often is attractive to him because she seems to care for him and understand him. Quite often she is considerably younger because at mid-life he is avoiding people his age who remind him that he is getting old. He likes to be with people who have youthful attitudes and ways of thinking.

YOUNG IS GOOD

He is sexually attracted to younger women whose bodies are still in shape and whose faces are not lined and weary.

YOUR DILEMMA

This doesn't seem fair to his wife, because there is little she can do to change her physical aging. Growing old is simply the natural result of living life—which they both have been doing, more or less together. After all, his body isn't the same trim, vibrant hunk it once was either. His face is also wrinkled, and his hair is getting gray and thin. However, while he is in the denial stage regarding his aging, he doesn't want to accept his own deterioration. Being with someone younger gives him some zip, and that feels good.

CAREFREE INTERLUDE

Because so many pressures are converging upon the mid-life man at one time, he consciously or unconsciously seeks relief. One of the ways he does this is by finding some carefree activity. Another woman can provide a casual atmosphere for your husband, because she doesn't have to discuss the running of the household or the family with him. She doesn't need to present him with the problems of the broken washer, your son's trouble in school, or the high dentist bill. She also doesn't have the problem of struggling with his neglect of her or his critical attitude. At this point, she hasn't lived with the history of his shirking family decision making, crabbing that your mother visits too often, or failing to keep his promises to go to your daughter's piano recitals. He presents his best side to her and doesn't do anything to threaten her acceptance of him.

Oh, he may claim that he has shared with her every miserable part of his life—his rotten deal at work, his unhappy relationship with you, his rebellious kids—and still she loves him. But he hasn't said things to belittle her or cause her personal anxiety. And she is very busy being the sympathetic listener to his woes, because in so doing she keeps his attention, and *she* needs that.

Another woman can provide some lighthearted breaks in a man's dreary, heavy world, at least initially. She doesn't have to share his responsibilities, and she is free to do "fun" activities with him. The excitement of getting to know someone new can be exhilarating and adventurous. The mystery of the unknown may be scintillating and be such a welcome contrast to the rest of his life that he is drawn in more and more deeply simply to experience relief from his oppressive burdens.

TIME TO SERVE HIMSELF

Many men have been living sacrifical lives for fifteen or twenty years. They have willingly accepted an increasing number of commitments at work, in the community, in the church, and—of necessity—with their families as they grew. By the time a man reaches mid-life, he is not only getting physically tired, but he is getting emotionally drained as well. When he thinks of ways of finding relief, he sees he is tied into obligations he cannot graciously escape, even for a little while. He feels trapped, and commitments he readily accepted at one time are now heavy, heavy burdens. He begins to get sick and tired of it all, and the need to escape becomes compulsive. A man is ready after all these years to serve himself for a change. After all, isn't it about his turn? Having an affair is part of this need to serve himself.

I am not giving excuses or permissions for affairs; I am stating reasons for them. If you really are going to understand your husband, you also need to comprehend the causes for an affair. That in no way means you approve.

I think of Henry, a Christian who decided he had denied himself recreation and pleasure long enough. For years he had put in almost double time in his profession, mostly to provide the good things in life for his family. He suddenly took up golf and spent every moment he could on the golf course. He worked much less but was away from home even more than before. His wife complained a lot but said she didn't care to join him when he once grudgingly suggested she come along. Before long Henry met a divorcee who did like to golf and their time together on the golf course led to an affair.

TOTTERING VALUE SYSTEM

Mid-life men are doing a lot of evaluating of what is important in life, and they are doing it at a time when they are emotionally low. Their value system gets a thorough shaking. They're not sure that their moral standards have been right. They may think it was unnecessary to have been so rigid. They may question biblical principles and commands on their lives. They may even wonder if a God-consciousness is important any longer. Right now they are confused and need to do a lot of sorting of values that have been an inbuilt code with them, a code they have been taking for granted for years.

When your husband is walking on this kind of unstable ground, he needs understanding and empathy. If you are preoccupied with other concerns or you scold him to "straighten up," he is a likely candidate for someone else's caring. If that someone else is a woman, a relationship may get started that ends with complications for all of you. Quoting Scripture verses to your husband about what is right and wrong is not going to be the kind of help he will accept. Scripture is not given to us as a weapon to use in clubbing someone over the head. It *is* given to us to use on ourselves, and now is the time to learn from the Bible about the best way of caring for your husband.

GROWING APART

Many mid-life marriages end in divorce because the couple decide they have grown apart. They simply don't have anything in common anymore. Their interests are widely divergent. As we have said, this separation usually has happened because the couple has not spent the necessary time together to keep in touch. They each have been busy succeeding in their careers—either in or out of the home. If those careers do not cross paths with each other, they become more distant from each other as they grow and develop in their specialties. A remedy for this is to spend much time all through your married life keeping each other up-to-date on your ideas and feelings.

Sometimes one mate participates in a class or some activity that starts a new self-awareness or self-development. If the other partner isn't involved in the activity, he may feel left out. It may not be possible for both to participate, but the participating mate should be sure to share how he is changing. Ideally, both mates should be finding ways to grow in their personal lives, and they should be sure to be communicating with each other about their growth.

We know of several couples in whose lives serious division has occurred because one spouse was growing and the other was not. Bob and Karen are a classic example. After several years of child raising and housekeeping, Karen started a small business that brought her in contact with many interesting people. At about the same time she began attending a weekly women's Bible study and started growing dramatically in her spiritual life. Before long she was using her business contacts as a means of sharing about Christ. This led naturally into many times in which Karen found herself counseling troubled people. She found fulfillment in being able to help. She also felt the need to get training in how to counsel, so she took an evening class taught by a local Christian psychologist.

There began to be a lot of tension between Karen and Bob. He was aggravated at her for the amount of time she was giving to her business and her classes, so if any of the housework was neglected, he pounced on her about it. Karen felt Bob was becoming narrow and stuffy, but when she suggested he take advantage of some ways to grow, he said he was too busy making a living. He felt her business wasn't much help to the family income, and he also felt that she was getting too high and mighty and looking down on him. Instead of appreciating the new ways she was expanding as a person, he felt threatened and picked on her. Karen found it easier to share her spiritual insights and other dimensions of her life with some close friends. Some of these friends also took time to have fun together. Because Bob didn't know them well, he always said he was too busy to join them. Karen decided not to stay at home with Bob but went with her friends for these social times, too.

Fighting between Karen and Bob increased. Bob was unwilling to understand and support Karen in her growth, and he felt no need to do any growing himself. Karen felt Bob was a shriveled, visionless person, and she was unwilling to give up the new fulfillment she had found. Their marriage has now ended in divorce.

In *Try Marriage Before Divorce*, James Kilgore points out that a married partner experiencing growth must recognize what complementary changes he is requiring of his mate as a result of his growth. The growing one must allow sufficient time for change to occur in the mate and for the adjustment to be integrated into their marriage. The other mate must be sure to be responsive to the input from the growing mate. Dr. Kilgore warns, "When a spouse feels good about what is happening in his life, but experiences rejection from his marital partner, the seeds of distrust are sown. As a pattern of lack of understanding develops, other sources more likely to be receptive and positive are sought."[1] Mid-life wives, tune in!

"POSSESS ME NOT"

Some mid-life men enjoy being with other women partly to prove that their wives don't completely own them after all. A wife's possessiveness does nothing to enhance their marriage and a lot to destroy it. A vicious cycle sets in—the more you clutch, the more your husband resists; the more he resists, the more insecure you feel and the more you clutch. A man's personhood is stifled when he feels possessed, and he may become angry. The anger may take many forms, and one of them may include involvement with another woman.

One of the greatest gifts of love is to give your husband the freedom to be himself. The granting of freedom doesn't mean that you condone immorality, but it does mean you recognize that he must make the choices for his life. To give your husband freedom doesn't mean you are indifferent or cold. It means you acknowledge his right to be a person. When you try to dominate his thoughts, his actions, and his will, you are setting yourself up as a god—and if you are honest, you will recognize that isn't your place. And if you free him to be himself, it doesn't mean he's automatically going to abuse the freedom. Don't let your clutchiness drive your husband away.

TROUBLE AT WORK

You may feel that your marriage has been good and that you generally are doing all the right things, but your husband has become a bear to live with anyway. One of the things to consider is his vocational stress. Marriage counselors find that there is a strong relationship between job satisfaction and marital fulfillment.[2] Often a man cannot control what is happening with his occupation, so he takes his frustration out on his family. His criticism of his wife and children may be attempts to gain control of at least some things in his life.

If the two of you handle vocational stress together, you can strengthen your union as you draw together against "an enemy." Too often, however, a husband battles his work problems alone. The hostility he directs toward his wife because of work stress can cause discord between them that grows into warfare. Kilgore observes, "We tend to let our occupational choices and stresses become buried in what appears to be more easily controlled experience. Numerous couples have been divorced because they failed to recognize the vocational stress that contributed to marital disharmony."[3]

Many factors may be involved in a mid-life affair other than a husband's simple, wanton lust. The reasons do not excuse the affair, but understanding the causes might help you do your part ahead of time so that an affair does not happen.

But suppose an affair is already taking place. How do you handle it? What will be your feelings and your responses to your feelings?

PAIN FOR YOU

One of the most common emotions resulting from a husband's affair is hurt. The hurt a wife feels is not only because a *younger* woman might be involved, but because *any* other woman is involved. A third party has been allowed to share in what was intended for only two. This can hurt as much as any physical wound and will need remedy and healing.

A wife may also experience anger, confusion, and self-pity. She may feel rejected, and her self-image may hit the zero line because she feels worthless. She probably cannot see any reason why her husband should do such a thing. She may become defensive and claim no part in the cause, or she may become overly self-blaming and tear herself apart with unreal guilt.

The emotional stages through which a wife goes when she learns of her husband's unfaithfulness usually are denial, reluctant acceptance, anxiety, grief, anger, and finally a determination to stay in or get out of the marriage.[4] The stages are similar to those we face with other tragedies in life and at death, and each stage needs to be adequately dealt with in order to reach peace at the end. To think that we can skip one or suppress it is a mistake. That particular emotion will surface again and usually in a more complicated, dangerous form. Experiencing each emotion is painful but necessary.

Donna's husband asked her for a divorce. Unknown to her, he and his secretary had been having an affair for years. He now told her, and he said he intended to marry the other woman. Donna refused to believe him and, in fact, would not believe any of her friends and relatives who verified the affair. She denied the situation so long without moving into the other necessary stages that when her husband completely moved out of the house and began living with the other woman without a divorce from Donna, she nearly went insane. She had always been an emotionally strong woman and a committed Christian, but her behavior became bizarre and she tried unsuccessfully to end her life. When she finally allowed herself to grieve and feel angry, she was able to begin to make realistic plans for her future and that of her children. She began to again think and act rationally.

EMOTIONS ARE NOT IMMORAL

Emotions such as anger, anxiety, and grief are normal and not in themselves wrong. How you *react* because of the emotions may be wrong, but you do not need to feel guilty because you have the feelings. Many Christians have carried a lot of irrational guilt for years because of the emotions they experience. I have learned that accepting my emotions as normal and not sinful has been liberating. What I do as a result of my emotions is another matter! Part of Christian maturity is learning to channel emotions into constructive, God-pleasing actions. I have found *Feeling Free* by Dr. Archibald Hart[5] and *Feeling Good About Feeling Bad* by Paul Warner[6] especially helpful, and I highly recommend them.

Concerning the directing of our emotions, Andre Bustanoby points out that anger, for example, can be handled either constructively or destructively.[7] Constructive anger generates the desire and energy to do something helpful about the problem. Destructive anger causes all sorts of harmful effects from cruel words to hurtful actions that often are regretted later and almost always complicate the original problem.

The hurt and anger a wife feels over her husband's affair or the imminent threat another woman presents are reasonable emotions. How she handles them will play a part in her husband's response to the whole situation. If she explodes all over the place and lowers the boom on him, she will probably drive him away. If she suppresses her feelings and tries to cover over her true reactions, those emotions will later erupt in some worse form, such as severe depression, attempted suicide, irrational behavior seemingly unrelated to the real cause, or a serious physical illness. If she assumes an uncaring attitude as a protection for herself, her husband will feel she doesn't care about him.

WHERE DO YOU GO FROM HERE?

If you have learned or suspect that your husband is having an affair, you need to be honest with yourself and with your husband. You need to acknowledge your feelings, but control them. You do not suppress nor stifle them, but you don't let them rage out of hand either. Rita R. Rogers, M.D., clinical professor of psychiatry at the University of California at Los Angeles advises, "The most important thing to do immediately is nothing. Don't flee into action, but rather retreat into reflection. Evaluate what it all really means—to him as well as to you."[8]

Other marriage counselors advise that you do not go into hysteria nor deliver hasty ultimatums. Keeping calm and working toward opening up communication with your husband bring the best results.

Richard Fisch, M.D., assistant clinical professor of psychiatry at Stanford University Medical School, says that every wife with an unfaithful husband must make a basic decision. "Decide whether you regard his extramarital conduct as such a fundamental abrogation of the marriage contract that it makes continuing the marriage untenable." Then, if you decide to stay in the marriage, "don't try to get him to confess the adultery through questioning, innuendo or other forms of entrapment. Tell him straight out that you know . . . and how you know." He also advises waiting until the first shock is over before you talk about it. When you do bring up the subject, "*don't* use threats, such as divorce or separation. *Don't* keep reminding him that you feel betrayed, that he has forever lost your trust.'"

GAMES WIVES PLAY

You must not play games either. When your emotions are all topsy-turvy, game playing is almost second nature. You may feel you are going to make your husband pay for what he is doing to you. Your actions and the very atmosphere surrounding you will then take on all sorts of vengeful connotations. Or you may feel so sorry for yourself that your tone of voice and mannerisms are oozing with misery.

Marian decided she was going to make her husband, Ted, pay for leaving her and living alone in an apartment while he tried to think things through. He still came home frequently to be with her and the children, and they sometimes had sexual intercourse while he was home, but he would always leave without staying overnight. She decided she was making things too easy for him by allowing him to have both the intimacy of family life and the privacy of his own apartment. She hastily decided to take the children and move out of state so they wouldn't be so convenient for Ted. They are now legally separated, and Ted is spending evenings and weekends with another woman and her children. Marian had really hoped Ted would beg her not to move and would promise to come home permanently. Many men have eventually returned home to stay, and marriages have been stronger than ever, when wives have been patient and have waited for them to be ready to come back. Marian's game went too far.

Kay, on the other hand, was the epitomy of self-pity when her husband started into his mid-life crisis. He never left her but one almost marvels that he didn't. Kay's voice whined. Her shoulders drooped as she dragged around the house, barely keeping up her work. She let her appearance go, no longer bothering to use makeup and seldom washing her hair. Her husband was unusually moody and withdrawn during this time, but Kay didn't try to find out why or volunteer to help him. She was too consumed with how he was treating her. He took longer than usual in making his mid-life transition, and neither of them grew much because of the experience.

You might take the tough, "I'll-make-it-no-matter-what" stance and your very being bristles with grit and determination. You may be going about wearing your "I-could-care-less" armor, or you may be the completely defenseless martyr sighing, "That's what I get in return for all I've given to him, but I'm still willing to die for him." Games cloud the real issue, so try to drop them by being as genuine as possible.

WHY DID IT HAPPEN?

You should try to discover why your husband had the affair, what the needs in his life were, what the attractions to the other person were, and what your part in remedying the situation is. You must go about this gently, however, and not use Gestapo tactics. You want to help restore the marriage, not seek revenge or prove how unjustly you've been hurt.

Wives are often surprised to learn that an affair doesn't happen because the husband is looking for better sex. He may have been looking for all the other kinds of attention you have not been giving. Assure your husband that you want to learn what his needs are and meet them. If he is in distress over his occupation, let him know that you will stick with him through any decision he feels he must make. He may want to use you as a sounding board to

71

think through steps he must take to change his work situation.

UNDERSTANDING IS CRUCIAL

We know that most men have trouble opening up about their feelings, and if your husband feels unhappy about his work, he may be afraid to admit it. He feels a heavy responsibility not to fail at his occupation or to provide for his family. James Kilgore says, "Faced with the idea of 'living up' to the expectations of others, few men have the courage to be something different, especially when the fear of failure in the new effort is strong. A wife who understands this struggle may be the greatest boon to personal growth a man has."[10]

Wanting to understand your husband, his problems, and his feelings may be one of the best keys to rebuilding your relationship. Since his crisis, my husband has often said that I was his best friend during that time. I was the one to whom he could talk when he felt like talking. He could let me know the very worst he was thinking and feeling, and I would still stick by him.

You may need to develop a new awareness of your husband's desires, reactions, and attitudes. This is done by practice. It helps me to think of "tuning in," much the same as finding the station I want to hear on the radio. The station is broadcasting over the airwaves all the time, but I don't hear it until I consciously turn on the power of the tuner and select the correct spot on the dial.

You can tune in to your husband by asking non-threatening questions, genuinely listening to all he has to say, empathizing, showing tenderness, encouraging and enabling him, and respecting him. Be sensitive to the timing of what you do. Don't force him to sit down "right now even if you are late for work" to start your question-

and-listen period. Be alert to when he is ready and circumstances are right.

WHO ELSE CAN HELP?

You may want to see a marriage counselor, but it is likely that your husband will not. Most men do not want to admit that they need help, because that looks as if they have failed. Do not harangue him into going, but perhaps he will agree to go at least once in order to help you with your needs. If you find a counselor who understands the mid-life situation and who develops a rapport with your husband, your husband may decide to continue marriage counseling. But don't be surprised if he doesn't.

There are many good marriage books available, and some of my suggestions are in the Suggested Reading List at the end of this book. One that is especially valuable for helping restore marriage is a book I've already quoted several times, *Try Marriage Before Divorce* by James Kilgore.[11] The author offers some good insights as well as very valuable do-it-yourself activities for husband and wife.

A Christian woman who has a marriage to restore must draw upon her resources in Christ. And you will need them all! It is so easy to let your humanness get in the way and take control. Being well acquainted with your Bible and drawing on the strength of its promises will be one of your biggest assets. There were times when I felt all I could do was hang onto the hem of the Lord's garments![12] I constantly needed to ask for the Spirit's help to prevent game playing, wrong motives, self-pity, and a host of other ills that wanted to take up residence in me. I needed to go to the Lord continually for a correct perspective on my problem.

SPECIAL FRIENDS

Having a human friend helps, too. In fact, having a real friend with whom you can share your problems will be vital to your ability to cope. You must be sure, however, that you don't simply use the friend as someone to gossip to about all your husband's faults. The friendship should be one in which you find strength to go on while you are in this wilderness. You need to be accepted by another human being and to know that you are still worthwhile. The friendship, however, should not take the time that you need to be spending with your husband.

A wounded wife needs an outlet, but some women spend so much time and energy "letting out" about their problems that they create new ones for themselves. They may neglect family and household, give too many personal details to too many people, and damage their husband's reputation so that it is nearly impossible for him to return to his former life. Dwelling on nothing but negatives will make chances of restoration dimmer and dimmer. The friendship should be one that encourages wholeness and helps you keep an objective view of your situation.

You should be sure that your intimate friendship is with a woman and not with another man. You are in special need of support and affirmation, and you may mistake male affirmation for love. Because you are experiencing a vacuum in your relationship with your husband at this time, you can easily fall prey to the attentions of another man, even though he may have initially intended only to help you. You need to remember that your husband's affair probably happened because of a vacuum *he* was feeling in his relationship with you. Since you are so desperately needing security at this disruptive time, you must not look for it from another man or you may find that you, too, have become involved in an affair. If you are part of a small group of caring Christians, you should be able to find support from them during this time. Small Bible study groups or other kinds of small groups should be alert to the needs of their members at all times and develop a climate of genuine love and caring. During special times of stress, such as the affair of one of the members' husband, that woman should be able to find affirmation and perspective from the members of her small group who will hold her sharing in confidence.

KEY RESOLUTIONS

A matter that must be totally settled is forgiveness. Before you can expect to see any change in your husband's actions or attitudes, you must decide whether or not you will forgive him for his unfaithfulness. Chapter 14 has more on forgiveness, but for now it is important that you adopt the attitude of Colossians 3:13: "Be gentle and forbearing with one another and, if one has a difference (a grievance or complaint) against another, readily pardoning each other; even as the Lord has freely forgiven you, so must you also (forgive)" (Amplified Version). If you know Jesus Christ as your Savior, you have experienced God's forgiveness. On the basis of God's having forgiven you, you are enabled to forgive your husband.

We know several marriages that have been preserved mainly because a wounded wife has been willing to forgive her husband. On the other hand, we know some couples who could have resumed a basically good marriage after an unfaithful husband repented and was willing to work on the relationship, but for various reasons his wife could not forgive. It is true that infidelity and desertion are scriptural grounds for divorce, but generally everyone in the family profits more from a restored marriage than a broken one.

If you have decided to work to save your marriage, draw upon God's strength and wisdom, control your emotions, totally forgive your husband, and use all the available resources for maintaining a proper perspective. You will also need patience. Your husband may or may not be ready to work on the restoration of his marriage. Even if he is willing, changes will not happen overnight. It takes time and pain to bring about the birth of a baby, and sometimes the development of a better marriage relationship is as long and laborious—and rewarding!—as the emergence of a new life.

Some of you may say, "Well, that's fine for other women, but it's too late for me—my husband has completely left me!" What do you do now?

8
LIFE WITHOUT HIM

The mid-life era has the second highest divorce rate of any time in married life. (The very highest rate is during the first five years of marriage.[1]) In addition to actual divorce and legal separation, however, there are also a great number of mid-life marriages that are broken by abandonment. The cause is usually a man's attempt to get relief from the tremendous pressures on him that are peculiar to this time in his life.

If your husband has left you and your family, you are probably going through one of the greatest trials of your life. You are probably experiencing the same emotions—rejection, hurt, anger, failure, and guilt—as the woman whose husband is having an affair. Your husband may not have left you for another woman, but he is gone nevertheless.

HIS REASONS

Many mid-life men leave home because they don't know

what else to do to relieve their tensions. They want to be alone to sort things through. They want to be free from the constant family demands they face when they are in the home. They don't feel like meeting anyone's needs, but when they are at home they feel guilty about not meeting the needs they see all the time. They want some peace of mind and some time to themselves without feeling constant guilt.

Some men leave home because they think that will be best for the family. They feel that they are so messed up and keeping life so confused for everyone that it would help the whole family if they just got out. Some men actually think they are going crazy and their family would be better off without them. What they don't realize is that their leaving causes more pain for the family than if they stay.

Some mid-life men, however, are actually driven out by their families. Their wives and children demand that they leave. In those cases, the wife is not too open for help, and the husband is the one who needs care and understanding.

FIT FOR THE GARBAGE HEAP

We have heard many true mid-life stories, but one of the most memorable was told to us by a man who really thought he must be going crazy because of his strange feelings and sometimes uncontrolled behavior. One night as he was eating dinner at home with his family, the sheriff arrived at his door with divorce papers and documents ordering him out of the house within one hour. His family was sitting right there and had never discussed a bit of this with him. They, too, had decided he was crazy and, without talking it over with him, had made arrangements to expel him.

The man was stunned! He gathered up some of his possessions and left. Convinced that he really was insane and worthless, he decided to end his life. He drove to a pawnshop and bought a handgun that the proprietor had to show him how to use. He decided to drive to the city dump to shoot himself. He felt so good-for-nothing, he thought the dump was a suitable place to leave his body. But when he arrived, the dump was closed and the gate locked. By now he was very distraught, but he knew of another dump that might be open. As he got back out on the highway, he was speeding and driving so erratically that a patrolman stopped him. The officer didn't notice the loaded gun on the seat beside him, but gave him a ticket for speeding.

Somehow that intervention of another person into his life was enough to cause the frantic man to step back into reality. He began to realize he didn't really want to kill himself and decided, "Hey, I can't be all that bad. Maybe I'm not as crazy as my family thinks I am." From then on, he began to get back his perspective and worked on his problems. His family never did take him back, however, and later his wife divorced him. He has tried to live as happy a life as possible, but now as an old man he feels he missed out on many of the good times he could have had with his children in their adult years.

Other men have told us their wives have laughed at them or chided them for breaking down and crying over their confusion about who they were, work problems, or any of the many other things men wrestle with in mid-life. After relentless berating or scoffing from their wives, many men have seen little alternative but to leave.

YOUR STRUGGLES

Whatever has caused your husband to leave—either your

79

persistent nagging, his own inner decision, or his desire to live with another woman—you and your children will face certain problems as you live without him in the home.

The anxiety of what the future holds is one of the greatest stresses. It is hard to trust the Lord with something so unpredictable as the outcome of your husband's absence. Your fear that he may never return, even though he might tell you his leaving is only temporary. As agonizing as this time is, it helps if you can keep looking at the "big picture." This time is only a part of the whole. Many men do return, and if they and their wives have each done some growing and correcting of the problems in their relationship, the marriage can be stronger than ever.

Al and Janet now have a strong marriage that is meaningful to both of them, but their relationship was on shaky ground during the worst time in Al's mid-life. Al moved out for several months, and although he was never involved with another woman, he was strongly tempted. Janet often felt anxious about the outcome, but she decided the surest way back for Al would be through her loving understanding and concern.

Jim and I became her confidantes and encouragers during this time. We urged her to assess what Al's greatest needs were and to try to meet those. She decided one of his needs was more time for relaxation. She knew he preferred to have her with him during his recreation, so she resigned from a volunteer position in the church so she could be with him. She also knew he would like her to share in handling the small accounting business he was building up on the side as a second income, so she took an adult education course in bookkeeping. When Al saw that she cared enough to make some adjustments for him, he soon came back home and was willing to work with her in rebuilding their marriage.

TIME TO GROW

Many women we know work on self-improvement while their husbands are gone. They take physical fitness programs, sewing classes, real estate courses, or piano lessons. They may read helpful books and work on getting rid of their habit of nagging. Often husbands find their wives more attractive because they do some growing and changing. Even if a husband isn't impressed or doesn't return home, a woman is a better, more fulfilled individual for having grown.

"But," you remind me, "I have my daily life to struggle through. I feel torn in pieces every waking minute. How can I carry on a somewhat normal life?"

That is where your dependence upon God comes in. He promises to be with you everywhere all the time. He is there to be leaned upon. He knows your heartache and bewilderment, and he wants you to pour out your heart to him.[2] He also wants to guide you step by step, and he offers his wisdom to you as he promises in James 1:5 and as we said in chapter 6.

Angie is one woman who has relied on the Lord to help her while her husband has been living in his own apartment. She often feels terribly hurt, but she has also found that God is a healer. Many times she has shared with me the new things God is showing her that help her understand her husband's problems and that assure her of God's love for her. Sometimes she is hit with a new disappointment, but she has learned to turn each situation over to the Lord and ask him to lead her.

Because you feel rejected by your husband's leaving, your self-image is no doubt suffering. You may feel worthless. You may feel that you are a failure in everything, including your marriage. You need to get your eyes off your troubles and look for what is still good.

When I get depressed about something, I find that turning my eyes away from my problems and to Jesus helps give me a balanced perspective once again. Take time to remember the good things about yourself and who you are because of God's grace.

You also need to do some things that make you feel good about yourself. Give yourself a fresh hairdo. Work on your favorite hobby. If you like to read, take time to read. Make time to be with friends so that you get some input from somewhere other than your own mind. Occasionally block out some time for your own rebuilding.

MORE HASSLES

If your children are living at home, you have their needs to consider. It is difficult to be both father and mother, especially when you are a *hurting* mother. As hard as it may be, you must give your children quality time. They need your support. It is *their father* who has left. Properly relating to your children at this time is so important that I have devoted the entire next chapter to the subject.

If your husband is not continuing to support the family as he did before he left, one of your major problems may be finances. If you were not already working outside the home, you may have to now. Finding a suitable job could be a big hassle and may also be hard on your self-image. If you quit work to get married or care for your children, you may find that younger women are handling your job with more skill than you now possess. You may find it difficult to get work hours that are convenient for your family, and you may find sexual discrimination in hiring and wages.

Lois was awarded a four-year scholarship to a university but gave it up to marry Ken. She had been more than willing to give herself as a wife and mother. Five children and nineteen years later she found herself divorced and with inadequate child support. She was forced to go to work but found she had few marketable skills so that she could earn what she needed. She had to take a job at minimum wage, be on her feet several hours at a time, and work many evenings and weekends when she needed to be with her children. She not only had the heartaches of divorce but had to cope with a very different life-style, unbearable fatigue, and neglected kids.

Relating to friends, neighbors, and relatives at this time may also be difficult because you feel embarrassed and uncertain. You need to be honest with your children, although how much you tell them will depend upon their maturity. You need to think carefully about what you're going to say so that they can handle it emotionally and not lose respect for their father. Although you need a friend or small group that can help you during this difficult time, be careful. It is better if the news of your husband's leaving doesn't travel to too many people immediately. Your husband will be able to come back more easily if fewer people know and people who do know, know very little. If your husband should want to return, he will be able to step back into his normal role and pattern of life with less struggle if he doesn't feel the whole world knows he left and is judging him for his "sins." If you are tempted to get revenge on your husband for his desertion by telling everyone, stop to think if you want him back. If you do, don't put up barriers he'll find impossible to hurdle.

YOUR CLAIMS

One of the first things that comes into your mind when

your husband leaves is the matter of your rights. After all, he is married to you and he "owes" you something!

True, he has responsibilities to you and the children, but demanding your rights will not ensure that you receive them nor will it help your relationship. That does not mean that you should go forever without seeking necessary financial support or finding an opportunity to discuss your other needs with him. Give him some time to heal first. Watch, too, how you approach him when you feel it is time. Remember that right now he is suffering from an overload of obligations. Your pressuring him about your rights will only make his struggle more acute. Giving him time to heal is similar to allowing someone time to recuperate from a physical injury or illness.

Chuck had left home and was living alone in a small apartment so he could have "peace and quiet and get his head together." He still supported the family financially and often telephoned or visited them. Evelyn felt lost without him at home as usual and was very angry about his leaving her with the heavy day-to-day responsibilities of four children. Every time he telephoned, she reminded him of his obligation as a father and husband. When he would come to visit, she would ask, "Are you ready to come home for good now?" If he took her out to dinner, she would turn the evening into a big hassle of discussing "their relationship." Chuck began to contact her less frequently and sometimes not at all for weeks. Then Evelyn gradually began to follow our advice and stopped putting so much pressure on Chuck. We reminded her that many wives would be delighted to have their husbands keeping in touch as Chuck was and that she should keep each contact time casual and friendly. As she did so, Chuck warmed up to her again.

But, you say, "He made a vow to me at the time of our marriage!"

That's true, but even Christians do not stay married because of vows they made at their wedding. That may shock you. If you can't trust a Christian to keep his word, who can you trust?

But remember that a mid-life man is often in such an emotional state that his own needs, which have gone unmet for decades, are stronger than the vows he made so many years ago. He may find it easy to explain away the binding nature of that ancient commitment because he is now questioning all his values.

INITIAL CHOICES

Those who counsel married couples find that people generally don't stay married because they made vows but because their current needs are being met. That may sound selfish, but documented research shows that all of us chose to marry on the basis of our needs.[3] Most of us were not aware of that when we chose to marry. One of the reasons friction develops in marriages is because these needs change as the years pass.

For example, your husband may have unconsciously chosen you because some of your traits met his need to be mothered. As he matured and perhaps grew more independent, and if you didn't withdraw the mothering, he has probably become irritated with your attempts to dominate him.

We know many men who have married sweet little girls who leaned on them for everything. The husbands liked this because it met their need to be a father. After several years of this dependency, the men grew tired of it and began to withdraw their attention. Then the sweet little girls became whiners, grasping for their husbands' care. Now their husbands would like more than anything for their wives to be independent and growing as healthy individuals. In fact, the whining and leeching drives some husbands right out the door! Their need for someone to depend on them for everything has changed.

DETECTING NEEDS

Because you and your husband have changed in many ways since you were married, your ways of relating should have changed also. Need changes are usually subtle, so lots of communication needs to be going on all through the marriage so that you stay current with each other. You do not grow at the same rates nor in the same areas, so you must keep sharing your ideas, interests, dreams, doubts, and your very selves with each other. If you are alert to your husband's particular struggles as he reaches mid-life, you can help satisfy some of his needs as he goes through this painful time of transition.

Some women ask, "What if my husband won't talk?" If your husband is still at home but doesn't talk about his needs, he may be afraid you won't understand or care. Some men have trouble talking about anything that is personal. Think of the situation as putting a puzzle together. Everything your husband does and says is a clue to his needs.

Other women say, "My husband has moved out. How can I learn what his needs are if I don't ever see him?" If your husband has moved out, you must piece together information about his needs from many sources. Spend some time with a close friend who knows both you and your husband and who can reflect on the past with you. The two of you may see some of your husband's needs that were always there but that you had ignored.

What do your husband's changed life-style, clothes, habits, and new friends tell you about some of his needs you may not have understood previously? If your husband is having an affair, the personality of the other woman should give you insight into some of his needs and also possible ways you might change. Any changes you make, however, must really fit you and not cause you to be uncomfortable with yourself. You can also learn what your husband's needs are by what his friends can tell you. Remember, you are not spying on him; you are learning who this man is so that when he takes another look your way, you will be ready.

THE OFFENDER'S DEBT

Some wives have asked us, "Do you think my husband realizes his sinfulness and the hurt he is causing me and the children?" They want to be sure their husbands feel guilty for leaving them. A natural human reaction is to want to strike back when we are hurt. Many wives want to be sure that their husbands are paying for what they are doing to them. They may not take any outward action against them, such as suing for divorce or forbidding them to enter the house. But they do everything within their power to make them feel guilty: "I can't get Amy to settle down at night. She keeps crying herself to sleep every night because she misses you." "Scott won't do a thing I tell him. And after all, it's not my place to keep after him about mowing the lawn or checking the oil in the car." "I have a terrible skin rash and haven't been able to sleep or eat, so the doctor wants me to get a prescription to quiet my nerves. But I don't see how we can afford that now."

Producing guilt, however, is not your job. It is God's. Your job is to make sure your own slate is clean and then to do what is necessary to restore your marriage. Reminding your husband of his sinfulness and his obligations to the family will not do anything to rebuild your relationship. Don't even pray, "God, make him see how wrong he is!" You *can* tell God all about your heartaches and then roll your worries and troubles over onto his shoulders. He promises that he watchfully and affectionately cares for you (1 Pet. 5: 7). You can also pray for the Lord to change *you* where you need it.

SUPER ANGEL

By now you may be saying, "Hey, that isn't fair! The husband is the one who has left home and may be misbehaving in all sorts of ways. Yet his wife is to be tolerant and accepting. She is to keep checking herself for right attitudes and actions and put herself out to be everything he needs. You are asking her to do double duty!"

I have said the same thing to my husband when I see the struggle some wives are going through to rebuild their marriage relationship. My husband, who has counseled hundreds of mid-life men and women during the past twenty-five years, admits that it isn't fair. But he has seen men return to their wives and their marriages restored when the wife has been willing to walk the second, and the twenty-second—and the two hundred twenty-second—mile.

You have to decide if you want to stay in your marriage. If you do, then you have to commit yourself, daily and minute by minute, to put up with a lot that is unfair as you do your part to correct the problems. You need a strong, vital relationship with the Lord so that you will feel his presence holding you up during the tough times. You will need a sensitivity to the guidance of the Holy Spirit when you don't know which way to turn next. You will need at least one good friend upon whom you can lean when the going gets too rough. Simply talking to someone else can help you get a new perspective and help you go on a little longer. You may need to be in touch with your friend very often during the hardest times.

HOW LONG?

If you don't eventually see results—and, in fact, you may see the situation worsening and taking on new and awful dimensions all the time—you may wonder how long to hang on. When should you give up hope? There does come a time to be assertive, and we will talk about that in chapter 11.

There may come a day when the situation is taken completely out of your hands. Your husband may sue for and win a divorce despite your efforts to prevent it. But wives are generally ready to give up too soon. And that is understandable. You are human and you get tired.

Exhaustion and frustration are the reasons why making contact with another human is indispensable. You need a friend who can be trusted to give you an accurate reading of the situation and who won't push you to get a divorce quickly. That person should not be easily biased to your side of the predicament but should try to have an overview of the total picture, including your husband's side. That friend should be able to give you the courage to keep on and to take hope.

FRIENDLY BALANCE

Martha often felt she was at the end of her rope during her husband's mid-life crisis, but her good friend Ruth helped her hang on. Ruth had gone through similar struggles with her husband a few years earlier, and she had learned that love and patience paid off.

When Martha got down too low, she could call Ruth and say, "I absolutely can't go through another night of wondering if Ed is going to come home. I think I just saw his car outside that big apartment building on Harris Street. What would he be doing there? I'm sure he's involved with another woman, and I can't stand that! This uncertainty is killing me. Maybe I'll just divorce him and end this frustration!"

Ruth had the right balance. She let Martha voice her feelings and anxieties and then gave her bits of wise advice. Martha would begin to feel calmer and see more clearly. "I'm so glad I can call you," she'd say. "Thanks for letting me unload and for giving me hope again."

If you don't have such a friend, then read your Bible more than ever, looking for verses that tell of God's love and help for you. If you are also continuing to read helpful books on personal growth and marriage relationships, you can get new strength and find ways to help yourself improve, which in the long run—win or lose your marriage—will be an asset to you personally. You may also enjoy reading lighter books and articles that are only for fun but will help to restore your equilibrium.

Situations differ for every family, but your family will experience one of three general situations if your husband leaves home. He may completely drop out of contact with the family. He may maintain some communication occasionally with at least part of the family. Or he may keep in touch regularly with phone calls and visits. His financial provisions may range from total support to no support at all.

THE DROPOUT

If your husband has dropped all communication with you or any of the family, your best course of action is not to chase after him. You may want to make sure he is well and safe, but after you know that, don't bother him. If you do, he may only run somewhere else. Or he may resent you even more. In some cases, depending upon his personality and the reasons for his leaving, a husband may need to know that you care for him and that he is welcome to return home. But don't pester him. Choose the best way to let him know that you care, do it, and then leave him alone. He will recover faster if you are not aggravating him.

THE DROPLET

The family who receives occasional contacts from a man who leaves, may feel wounded every time. You need to pray that God will give you special grace whenever he contacts you so you can be wise, patient, and loving. Each time your husband gets in touch with you, you are being tested. How you handle the encounter will have a lot to do with the decision he is making about whether or not to return. Again, it may not seem fair. You are under unusual stress, and yet you need to be at your best emotionally and spiritually. That is why you need to keep in vital fellowship with the Lord and some human friends.

THE DROP-IN

The man who keeps in frequent touch by telephoning and visiting seems to get to eat his cake and have it, too. He gets to have the benefits of home and the benefits of independence. Some men who have left will walk unannounced into the house, sit down to meals, watch tv, help themselves to the food in the refrigerator, play with the children—and leave again.

You don't need to feel that you are being used and abused. Show that you want to be his best friend and provide what he needs during this time of his confusion.

91

Be sensitive to whether or not he feels like talking. But don't pressure him into deep conversation, especially about where your relationship is now, when he is coming home, and so on. It is a good sign that he at least keeps coming to the house for short times. Women who never see their husbands would like to trade places with you.

SURVIVAL TACTICS

One of the best things for a wife whose husband has left, whether temporarily or indefinitely, to do is to study his needs and what made him leave. As you learn more about your husband and what he is experiencing right now, you will know better how to meet his needs when you have the opportunity. But be sure they are his real needs and not simply what you think they are.

Suppose I want to show Jim I love him and am trying to meet his needs. He has been so busy lately that he doesn't get to keep our lawn cut as he used to do. I am embarrassed by its unkempt appearance, so I arrange to have several loads of decorative stone delivered and spread over the yard. Now he'll no longer have to mow the lawn!

The problem is that Jim dearly loves green grass and growing things. He feels more relaxed in an outdoor setting. His real need is to have the grass, mowed or unmowed. I have to know his likes and dislikes, his values, and his feelings well enough to meet his true needs.

Or suppose that Mary notices Joe would rather stay home and watch tv or work on a hobby than spend time with their friends as they have usually done several times a month. If she learns from him that right now he is bothered by the noise and clamor of groups and wants some time to unwind without feeling responsible to anyone, she will wisely allow him that time. His need is to be quiet and have time for reflection.

Another thing for you to do is to evaluate where you

need to strengthen your life. While you are going through this period, do what you can to grow personally and to develop talents and abilities you may have been neglecting. If you have been a leaner, learn now to be more independent. (You may have to, anyway.) If you have been a nagger, think of alternate ways of handling the situations that make you nag. If you have been careless about tuning in to your husband's needs, try to develop a keener sensitivity to everyone you know. Take up a new hobby, enroll in an adult education course, or learn a new skill. Most husbands admire their wives for doing something to grow and develop, if they aren't neglecting other important responsibilities. What you choose to learn or get involved in may also be something your husband is interested in.

But the most important thing for you to do is to practice patience. When it seems there is no change in your situation, be patient. When you wonder how much longer you can hold on, be patient. That doesn't mean you have to be a doormat and be trampled on. It does mean that you will keep trying every way possible to restore your marriage. It means that you will work on the things you need to improve about yourself. It means that if you have the opportunity, you will work very carefully at communicating with your husband in loving ways and not pressure him in any way. *And you keep practicing patience.* There are times to take positive action; we will talk about how to do that as we discuss assertiveness in chapter 11. Before you take that step, however, take every other step you know of to help your husband—and yourself—survive his crisis.

WILL IT PAY OFF?

You may wonder if your patience and your efforts to do

all the right things will ever bring your husband back. No one can say for sure. But everything you do to help him at this time increases the chances of your marriage being restored. You and your husband have a history of life together that is going to be meaningful as he weighs whether or not to stay in the marriage. His ties to his children are another magnet. In spite of all the friction that is common to family life, most people still have a desire to be in families. Your husband may want freedom from his heavy family responsibilities for a while, but eventually he will want to be part of a family again.

If your husband is involved with another woman, another factor in your favor is that she probably will begin to make demands on him. She will push for him to get free from you and make a more solid commitment to her. The carefree atmosphere of their relationship will come to an end. The novelty of the new experience will wear off. If you have been growing and making positive changes, your husband may find you and the home life you symbolize increasingly desirable. Remember that his mid-life crisis is temporary. Statistics favor the likelihood of a marriage restoration if you are understanding and work at it. Hang in there!

In the meantime, while your husband is gone or if there's turmoil with him at home, what do you do about your children?

9
LIFE WITH THE CHILDREN

While your husband is in the midst of his mid-life crisis, you may not be sure if your children are a blessing or a curse! If you didn't have them, your husband would not have so many obligations and feel the pressure to keep going in a job he hates. You, too, would have more freedom. Perhaps you would have been a more attentive wife all these years if you hadn't had to spend so much time with the children.

On the other hand, you know you wouldn't give up the kids for anything! They are a joy to you and they provide some of the companionship you need during this lonely time. You must make sure, however, that your relationship with your children doesn't become a substitute for your relationship to your husband.

Life with your children, no matter what their age, gets

complicated if your husband begins an affair, leaves you, or both. How much you tell them about the situation depends upon their emotional maturity. You need to be honest, and yet you need to spare them the details. You should not drag them through the whole gamut of your emotions.

TUNING IN

You need to realize that your children also are hurting. They need time to adjust to the new situation. Even adult children living away from home suffer a loss when there is a tear in their parents' relationship. Jim and I have recently interviewed a number of university students whose parents had divorced within the past five years. Their comments about family friction indicate how deeply children are affected by marital trouble between parents. For instance:

"I can't even study. I just sit and wonder what went wrong with my parents."

"I hurt so bad that I can't stand to even think about my dad."

"I feel so lost and separated from my parents and my brother and sisters, too. It's as if I've been divorced, too."

"I feel cheated. I feel I don't even know what a good wife should be like."

One young man said, "After learning of dad's affair, I'm terrified of marriage and can't even think of having intercourse because of love."

"My dad tells me he loves me, but I find that hard to accept after what he did to my mom."

"I feel like I don't have a home anymore. I guess none of us kids matter to my folks."

Vigeveno and Claire, who work with children from broken homes, remind us, "Healing is not instantaneous.

The deeper the wound, the longer it takes to heal, and this disruption in the home is not a little scratch but a very deep wound."[1] These authors are talking about divorce, but even if your husband has left the home without divorcing you, the disruption is still intense and so is the uncertainty of what will happen next.

Young children often blame themselves when their father leaves. You need to reassure them that they did not cause him to go. They also fear that you might go, too. They feel helpless and are very frightened about being abandoned, so they need to know that you aren't going to leave them. They may not verbalize their fears, but you need to tell them often that you will stick with them. You need to be alert to what is going on in the minds of your children, whatever their ages, and open up the opportunities for them to talk. This is a difficult time for everyone in the family, but open communication and caring for each other will ease the pain somewhat.

SUPER MOM

To give your children the kind of emotional support they need, you will need to give them your time. You may be busy with a job and many more responsibilities than before, so you will have to work hard at providing this. However, good quality time with your children is one of the most important items to program into your schedule. Teens need your emotional support as much as do younger children.

Touching your children with lots of hugs and love pats will be reassuring during this time of stress. Teens need to be patted and hugged, too. Look for opportunities to put your arm around your child's shoulders and say, "I am really proud of what a great person you are growing up to be!" Touching will help your children to feel good about themselves and assures them that you are not going to desert them.

Be sure you don't undermine your husband's reputation with the children when you are explaining what is happening. They need to respect him and to continue to love him. You can let them know the facts about what is happening between you and your husband without burdening them with details or running down your spouse. If your husband returns home, life will be much easier for him and the children if they haven't come to hate him. Help them try to understand him.

You also are setting a pattern for them to follow when they have troubles in their interpersonal relationships. If they see you showing genuine love and kindness to your husband, they will be more apt to do the same when there are hard times with their friends or with each other. Let them hear you pray for dad's safety and for God to show him his plan for him. The entire atmosphere of the home will be healthier if you practice peacemaking and kindness in your speech and in your actions.

IDENTITY CRISIS

This time is crucial in the self-esteem of your children. How you talk about your husband or what they hear you say to him will affect their image of themselves. Vigeveno and Claire state, "Even though boys tend to be protective of their mothers, their self-esteem is linked to their fathers. Girls often feel sorry for daddy because he lives alone in an apartment. But if her father makes derogatory statements about her mother, then the daughter's self-image is affected because she identifies with her mother."[2]

Studies by the authors of *Surviving the Break-Up: How Children Actually Cope with Divorce* show that the best adjusted children have a stable, loving relationship with both parents and receive regular visits from the absent parent that the parent in custody encourages.[3]

For your children's well-rounded development, exposure to good parent models of each sex is needed. If your husband has left, you need to involve your children with male relatives or friends. Teens, especially, need to be around married couples who have a strong relationship so that they get a good perspective on their future roles.

Often children and teens get into serious trouble at school or with the law when the home is in upheaval. You will need to understand the cause of the behavior and be as objective as possible in finding solutions. You cannot flippantly excuse the child's wrongdoing. Neither can you be unjustly harsh. What you need to do is provide security for your child even though your relationship with your husband may be very insecure. Chapters 5 and 6 of Andre Bustanoby's *But I Didn't Want a Divorce*[4] and the book *Divorce and the Children*[5] have very good helps for meeting children's needs, even if your marriage hasn't ended in divorce.

THE PROTECTION TRAP

If your husband has left or if there is lots of turmoil in the home with him there, avoid the pitfall of overprotecting your children. You will tend to do this to compensate for the upheaval. You are sorry about the emotional harm they are experiencing, so you want to keep them from other dangers. Some mothers move their children into the same bedroom with them. Others won't let their children go anywhere without them.

If this goes on for an extended time, you may keep them from having experiences they need to grow up and develop confidence in themselves. They still need to be with friends and to attend church and school activities.

The opposite of overprotection is to let them go completely unsupervised. Some women are so wrapped up in their own problems that they aren't aware of their children's activities. Not knowing where they are or what they are doing is dangerous—for them. They need to know you care enough about them to be concerned. I used to think that was simply a neat philosophy to keep parents doing what they ought to, but as our daughters got into junior high and senior high, they used to point out kids they felt sorry for because their parents gave them so much liberty they felt unloved.

GUIDELINES GIVE PEACE

As difficult as it may be for you to get outside of your own troubled mind, you need to stay close to your children, their needs, and their comings and goings. You need to maintain those firm guidelines you established regarding their behavior. If your guidelines aren't firm, you need to work at clarifying the limits within which your children can function and then see that they stay within those limits. Children out of control will only multiply the problems you already have.

If your children have already experienced too much freedom and you realize that you need to change the situation, you now will need to do it carefully and gradually. If you suddenly start cracking the whip, your children are apt to feel that dad's departure has brought this on. Since they already are in an emotional upheaval, sudden and stern discipline may cause them to rebel, become very distraught, or suppress their suffering so that it will crop out in serious problems later. So if you need to do some shaping up in family discipline and behavior, do it gently and gradually, but firmly and consistently. Don't forget to include the children in the planning of the guidelines. And give them plenty of explanation when you need to enforce those guidelines.

Another danger during this time is that of spoiling your children with material possessions and privileges you wouldn't ordinarily allow. When you feel guilty because your marriage isn't running as smoothly as you feel it should, you may want to make it up to them by indulging in treats, toys, clothes, and activities that are far more excessive than your usual family standards. You may also think you are buying their allegiance so they'll be on your side instead of your husband's. The only person getting fooled is you. Even very young children know the trick, and they can work it well to their advantage.

KEEP IN TOUCH WITH GOD

It is easy to fall into the trap of letting your family's spiritual life grow cold, too. You may question God's love for you in allowing this mess to happen. You just may be so confused and frustrated that you feel you aren't getting through to God in prayer. Your state of mind prevents you from understanding anything in the Bible. If there has been a lot of yelling and bad feeling in the house, you may feel hypocritical to suggest it is time to pray or have family devotions. You may be embarrassed to go to church. Or the children's friends at church may say cutting things to them about what has happened. So you stay away.

Remember that neglecting your relationship with the Lord is a *trap*. Satan makes you feel worthless so you won't come close to the Lord. He makes you doubt God's goodness and power. Then you feel lonely and even more guilty. You forget to ask God for wisdom, and you go bulldozing around with your own ideas and your own

YOUR DILEMMA

strength. Your children pick this up, and soon the whole family may be on the outs with God. You need to remind yourself of God's love. Reread such passages as Ephesians 1, Romans 5, and Psalms 23, 103, and 139. Do the things that maintain your fellowship with the Lord so you can be an example to your children. Pray and share Scripture together and talk about God's help and care for you. Don't let Satan deprive you of your best source of strength at this time. Properly guiding your children is a superhuman task, even under the best of circumstances. Let God work within them and within you to make the way smoother.

PRACTICAL POLICIES

I have found Vigeveno and Claire's "Guidelines for Building a Happy, Harmonious Single-Parent Home" so practical and helpful that I include them here. They are useful for two-parent homes, too!

Basic Attitudes–What kind of an atmosphere do we want to create in our home?

1. What is our main emphasis as a family? How will we change or strengthen this?
2. What am I telling the world and my children about myself by my life-style? How will I change or strengthen this?
3. What kind of memories will we all have as a result of living together in a single-parent home?
4. How can we become better listeners to each other?
5. Do we allow each other freedom of speech and the right to express different opinions?
6. Is our home a place of love? Of respect? Of courtesy? Of good manners?

Standards and Rules–Does everybody know what is expected of him as a member of this family?

1. What time is bedtime on school nights? On weekends?
2. How much television time can we allow each day?
3. How much time do we need for homework each day? How much does mom or dad get involved in homework?
4. What books and magazines will we have in our home? What reading material will not be permitted?
5. What family standards will we adopt for movies?
6. How will we handle issues such as alcohol, cigarette smoking, marijuana, etc.?
7. How much freedom can the teenagers in our home handle? What freedoms will they have?
8. When an adult is not at home, are the children and teenagers allowed to invite their friends into the house? Girls? Boys?
9. Do we agree on standards for clothes, hair, language? What compromises will we make?
10. What are our nutritional standards? Will we make any changes?
11. Do we say grace before meals at home? In restaurants?

The Parent's Responsibilities—What do I need to do to help my children mature?

1. How can I help my children be prepared for adulthood by the time they are legally adults?
2. How can I teach self-reliance?
3. What are my guidelines for discipline?
4. How will I reinforce good behavior? Discipline bad behavior?
5. How can I help my children develop their individual interests?
6. How can I deal with boredom when a child complains that there is nothing to do?
7. How will my children get their spending money? By allowance? By earning it? By need?
8. How will household responsibilities be delegated— chores inside the house; in the yard; training, feeding

and cleaning up after pets; etc.?

Parental Guidelines–Am I Prepared to lead my family along established guidelines?

1. Will we attend church as a family? How many meetings a week or how many church activities can we handle as a family? As individuals?
2. Will we have family devotions? Encourage personal devotions?
3. What will our weekend be like? How much time will we set aside for chores? Family activities? Individual activities?
4. How will we celebrate birthdays? Holidays? Have I considered my children's mother/father, grandparents, aunts, uncles and other relatives on special days of the year?
5. Am I able to handle my finances? Should I budget my money? Can I afford credit cards? Is it necessary to cut expenses?
6. Can I teach self-control by example? How can I strengthen my own self-control?
7. When will I discuss sex with my children? Am I prepared to answer their questions about sex?
8. Who can I turn to in times of crises that can help me?[6]

LET CHILDREN HELP

During your husband's mid-life crisis, whether or not he has left you, enlist your children to help. No matter what their age, they can help keep their father's stress to a minimum.

My husband went through a time when he could no longer stand the phone ringing, people coming to the door, or making decisions regarding our youngest daughter, then a high school student. Becki and I went on a campaign to reduce tension as much as possible for him. We answered all the phone calls and steered people who needed Jim to other sources of help. If Becki's friends came to see her, we kept them in another part of the house away from Jim. We tried not to hassle him with decisions about where she could go, what time she should be in, and so on. As he began to mend, he was gradually able to be involved again, but we needed to protect him temporarily.

Children can keep down noise, turn off the music dad doesn't want to hear, and in general keep tension to a minimum. It is good for them to practice being caring and unselfish. You can lead them to think of helpful things to do—a surprise car wash, the lawn mowed, or a special meal. Dad may not seem to notice, and he may even appear ungrateful, but teach the kids not to be discouraged. Tell them that someday he'll appreciate what they're doing. He will!

Our daughters were in their teens and early twenties when Jim was in the midst of his crisis. Barbara and Brenda were away at college, and Becki was still at home. They were very sensitive to his problems. In fact, they were sometimes able to be more alert to his needs than I was. They wrote him encouraging notes, showed him affection, and did and said many things to let him know they respected and loved him. Barbara cancelled plans for spending the summer out of state because she knew dad was already grieving that she and Brenda had to be away at college during the year. She had counted on the out-of-state experience for a long time, but she decided she needed to be around home to encourage dad. As it turned out, she was also a big encouragement to me.

All three girls were a help to me during this time. They occasionally offered to take over the house so I'd be free to spend time with Jim. They said things to me that raised my sagging self-esteem. They offered to do things with me, such as go shopping or bike riding. They seemed to look for ways to be special friends to me.

HOLDING ON TO DAD

Your children can be enlisted to pray. They can pray specifically that God will take their father successfully through this tumultuous time in his life, that God will show him what to do about his work if that is a problem, that God will help him find more leisure time, and that he will help with whatever their father's needs are.

Our daughters prayed often for God's help for their dad. Often on Sunday mornings when Becki and I would be at home hurrying to get dressed for church, Jim would call from his church study to tell me he didn't think he could possibly make it into the sanctuary to preach that day. He felt like a hypocrite, preaching about God's power and concern for everyone and feeling as if it weren't real in his own life. In fact, he was sure that he wouldn't be able to hold out any longer against the compulsion he had to run away. Each time after he would call, Becki and I would stop everything to pray. Claiming the promise in Matthew 18: 19 that "if two of you agree down here on earth concerning anything you ask for, my Father in heaven will do it for you," we would plead with God to deliver Jim from his pressures, reassure him of God's love, and enable him to go on with life. Having Becki to pray with me had a lot to do with bolstering my own faith and ability to believe that God would eventually bring Jim through this wilderness. Those prayer times also helped Becki to grow spiritually.

Your children can be a *blessing* to you—and to your husband—during this time!

PART 3
HELP FOR YOU

10
PEACE THAT EMPOWERS

Helping *you* live through your husband's mid-life crisis is one reason this book is being written. I mentioned earlier that as soon as my husband's book *Men in Mid-Life Crisis* was put on the shelves for sale, we began to get calls from all over the United States from women who needed additional help. The very first call came from the owner of a bookstore, a lady whose husband was apparently experiencing mid-life crisis. She read the book the moment it came into her store.

Letters and telephone calls continue to come from wives with more questions about how they personally can manage during their husbands' mid-life crisis and how they can help their husbands survive. When Jim and I speak at conferences or on radio and television talk shows about the man's mid-life crisis, a large portion of the questions people ask are about how a wife can help her husband and how she can cope personally.

Men in Mid-Life Crisis was written to help both men and their wives understand the problem, and Jim specifically wanted men to find help for themselves through the book. By acknowledging the problem and learning that it is common to most mid-life men, many men have been able to start working on the necessary tasks of this transition time. That book gives men some very practical help.

This book is designed to give you wives the same kind of practical help. We have set the stage by discussing your husband's problem and how it affects you. We have also talked specifically about your response if your husband should have an affair and/or leave the home and how you should respond to your children during this time. Now we want to discuss the strengths you have to draw upon and how you can personally live as successfully as possible while your husband goes through his mid-life crisis.

PEACE WHILE UNDER FIRE

The foundation for inner strength at any time in your life is your relationship with God. You are strongest when you are experiencing inner peace. That peace comes only from being in touch with God. Circumstances around you may be very *unpeaceful,* but you still can enjoy a solid, calm power within yourself. Of course, you cannot simply say, "OK, I'll forget the mess things are in and be peaceful!" You have to meet some basic requirements before you can experience peace.

Inner peace comes from Christ, not from exerting your will and determining to be peaceful nor from ignoring the situation around you. Jesus said, "Peace I leave with you; My peace I give to you; . . . Let not your

110

heart be troubled, nor let it be fearful."[1] He also said, "These things I have spoken to you, that in Me you may have peace. In the world you have tribulation, but take courage; I have overcome the world."[2]

To qualify for peace, you must be in Christ. To be *in Christ* means that you have accepted him as your Savior. You recognize that he gave his life to redeem you, and you certainly need to be redeemed![3] When you acknowledge your sinfulness and then appropriate God's forgiveness and cleansing through Christ's death, you are accepted into God's family.[4] Being in God's family means that you share in the inheritance, and part of that inheritance is God's peace.[5]

Being in Christ means that you have been born again.[6] You have new life in Christ for your present existence[7] and you have eternal life for the future.[8] In order to claim a relationship with God, you need the rebirth that comes from accepting Christ as Savior. For some of you this is old news, but for others it will be new, or perhaps you've never before paid any attention to it. For each of you, however, this is *good news,* and it needs to be appropriated into your personal life. It is necessary for your eternal good as well as for more successful living now.

FELLOWSHIP IS ESSENTIAL

Once you are a "born again Christian," you will want to keep in vital fellowship with the Lord so that his strength and peace can flow into you. You keep in fellowship with the Lord much the same way as you keep in contact with a human friend. You talk to each other, you spend time together, and if you do something to offend your friend, you ask his forgiveness. If you want to be close friends with God, do the same. The more time you spend with God, the better you will know him.

What do you do when you spend time with the Lord? The ultimate, of course, is to realize that God is with you all the time and you can hold a conversation with him at any time. You can practice a "God consciousness" so that in everything you do and say you are aware that the Lord is involved.

You will also need to have special times with the Lord when you put aside all other duties and thoughts. Your life is probably jam-packed with busyness, so you will need to schedule a regular meeting time with God each day. Be sure you keep that appointment! It is a vital, life-maintaining time for you. Imagine that your physical life is only sustained by regular hookup to a kidney machine. Then apply that same principle to your spiritual life. Your spiritual health depends upon a periodic and frequent hookup with God.

During those special times with God you should ask the Holy Spirit to teach you. God's Spirit can make the Bible understandable and meaningful to you. You need to read enough of the Bible each day to find some thought to apply to your life and the problems you are facing. If you have time for a thorough study, that is great. Use a concordance and several Bible translations. Jot your findings in a notebook. If you don't have a long time to study, at least read a portion of Scripture. It is better to read a little than none at all because you don't have time for a detailed study. New readers should not start at the beginning of the Old Testament and try to read the Bible straight through. You will get bogged down when the genealogies start! Begin by reading the Gospels in the New Testament, and then perhaps 1 John, Acts, Ephesians, Colossians, Philippians, and James, and then Psalms and Proverbs in the Old Testament. Use a modern translation of the Bible so that the language doesn't get in the way of your understanding.

AS NECESSARY AS BREATHING

Prayer should be a part of each special time spent with God. I find it helpful, first of all, to focus on God, his character, his great power, and his great love for me. That leads me to a confession time, because I realize how unfit I am to come before him until I have admitted my sins and accepted his cleansing through Christ.[9] However, I know that because of Christ I now have the privilege of coming to the Father with boldness.[10] That causes me to spend time praising and thanking him specifically for who he is, what he has done for me, and for particular things he is bringing about in my life. Then I move to a time of petition for others' needs and for my needs. Whole books have been written on prayer, and if you need more help with how to pray, be sure to read some of them which are in the Suggested Reading List at the end of the book.

During your husband's mid-life crisis, you might pray specifically for God to show you definite ways in which you should meet your husband's needs and for God's power to help you change. Then you put feet on your prayers by working on the changes! You might need to control your tongue. Ask God each day, or even several times a day, to help you not to speak when you shouldn't and to speak appropriately when you should. You might need to spend more time listening to your husband. Ask the Lord to help you be attentive and to arrange your work so that you have time alone with your husband.

After you have asked God for the things that need to be changed or strengthened in your own life, you can pray for your husband's needs. But *don't* ask God to straighten him out. Instead, ask the Lord to give him physical rest and mental refreshment. Ask also for your husband to be kept strong against temptation. Ask God to make his

113

presence very real to your husband so that he experiences joy and relief from those pressures that have become so intolerable to him.

PRAY FOR "WHO?"

Are you ready for this next suggestion? Pray for the "other woman" if there is one in your husband's life. That's a big order for you, but you will find that praying for her will be a step toward your own emotional wholeness. Ask God to bring her to a true knowledge of himself, if she is not a Christian. If she is a Christian, pray for the Holy Spirit who dwells within her to guide her thoughts and decisions, especially regarding her relationship to your husband. Also ask God to meet her needs. Remember, there is a reason why she needs what your husband is giving her.

Pray for the Lord to guard your children against the instability that exists in your home right now. Pray for them to continue to grow in every way that is best for their maturation spiritually, emotionally, educationally, and socially. Ask God to give them an understanding of what their father is experiencing.

God invites you to pour out your heart to him. Psalm 62: 8 says that we are to trust him all the time for he can help. If your best human friend were wise enough to know what you need right now and strong enough to provide it, you would be sure to hold frequent conversations with that person. God *is* that wise and all-powerful friend. Be sure to talk to him often.

EXPECT TO GROW

When you keep in close contact with the Lord over an extended period of time, you will notice that spiritual and emotional growth have taken place. You should be able to look where you were six months ago and see areas in which you have improved. Sometimes the progress is slight and you may not be able to recognize growth easily in yourself. Be assured, though, that you are growing and developing as you allow the Lord to work in you.

A sure sign of growth is fruit, and Galatians 5: 22 tells us, "But when the Holy Spirit controls our lives he will produce this kind of fruit in us: love, joy, peace, patience, kindness, goodness, faithfulness, gentleness and self-control; . . ." Each year you live as a Christian there should be indications that you are more loving, more joyful, more peaceful, more patient, kinder, more filled with goodness to others, more faithful, gentler, and more self-controlled. You will need a bountiful harvest of every one of those qualities during your husband's mid-life crisis!

Another sign of your growth will be that your commitment to the Lord will grow stronger. As you see him faithfully working in your life, you will realize that you can trust him more. Now, during your husband's trauma, you may sometimes feel you have to look very hard to see God working. Probably that is because you are expecting God to work at your rate of speed or on the things you have outlined for him to do. You can't tell God what to do, but you can commit your concerns to him. As you turn over more areas of your life to God, your confidence in him will grow.

GOD'S CHARACTER

Confidence in God comes about when you grow in your understanding of him. You might like to make a study of God's characteristics. As you search the Bible you will see that he is perfect love, completely just, absolutely sinless,

115

the ultimate in wisdom, and all-powerful. Add all the other superlative qualities you can think of. You will see that he is worthy of your worship and your confidence. As you keep walking with him in your daily life, you will sense that he loves you personally and is in control of this world. Yes, there is a battle going on between good and evil, God and Satan. But you know God is going to be the ultimate victor. He sees that "all that happens to us is working for our good if we love God and are fitting into his plans" (Rom. 8:28).

As you grow in your Christian life, you will see more clearly how Scripture relates to every area of life. This means that you need to be familiar with the whole Bible so you can incorporate more of it into your life-style. Don't be discouraged if at this point you aren't well acquainted with the Bible. The time to get started knowing more is now. Study the Bible for more than content. Read it to see how you can apply the principles to your life *today*.

ACCEPTING OR REMAKING?

Growth in your spiritual life is also marked by the way you relate to others. The more mature you become, the more sensitive you should be to the needs, joys, trials, and feelings of the people around you. You should be more unselfish and more understanding of others as you grow in your personal understanding of God. As you see that God accepts you just as you are, you can accept others as they are—without your remaking them first.

You probably know people who make you feel uncomfortable because they want to impose their ideas and beliefs on your life. I think of a woman who always had conditions on her friendship with me. She tried to do my thinking for me. "You don't really let your kids play in the rain, do you?" Or, "Well, if I were you, I'd tell my husband he shouldn't spend so much time at the church." If I tried to disagree with her, she got a sour, disgusted look on her face that was intended to punish me or make me feel stupid. When one person relates judgmentally to another, the friendship is stifled. When you accept someone, it doesn't mean you condone or condemn his beliefs, values, or actions. It means you allow him to be his own person.

Your spiritual growth will enable you to work at loving others. Yes, I said "work." Real love is not an involuntary feeling that sweeps over you. Real love is commitment. John Powell tells us that genuine love is when two people "are willing to acknowledge and respect *otherness* in each other. Each person values and tries to promote the inner vision and mysterious destiny of the other. Each counts it his privilege to assist in the growth and realization of the other's vision and destiny."[11]

SPECIAL NICHE

Another sign of your growth is that you will become increasingly aware of your mission in life. When you know God more fully and relate to others unselfishly in love, you will sense God's purpose for you more keenly. As you evaluate the gifts and abilities God has given you and the opportunities he presents for using them, you will know that God made no mistake when he created you to be the person you are. You are unique. You are the only person in the world just like you. No one else comes from the same position in the same family, from the same geographical area, with the same childhood experiences, with the same educational background, or with the same adult experiences. God has been putting into your life exactly the talents, events, and people he wants to make you what he wants you to be. Your job is to let the potter mold you into the vessel he has in mind.

A lot of people through thoughtlessness or under the guise of humility have never realized the abilities they possess. You may feel that if you aren't a great pianist, soloist, or seamstress, you have nothing worth calling a talent. Did you know that being a good listener is as valuable as being a great stage person? Taking soup to someone who is sick is as important as preaching a mighty sermon! If you are not a leader, you can be one of the best, most cooperative helpers there is! The busy mother who can spend an extra half hour a day praying is as necessary as the lady who directs the church Christmas program. God has special things to be done in some people's lives that only you can do.

SPECIAL NEEDS

There are certain spiritual qualities that you will need especially during your husband's mid-life crisis. We have mentioned some of them throughout the book but let's list them, along with others, here:
- Complete trust in God
- Genuine love for others, especially your husband and children
- Kindness
- Serenity
- Patience
- Acceptance
- Wisdom and discernment
- Openness
- Honesty
- Selflessness
- Self-control
- Endurance

I'm sure there are many more qualities we could list, but if you are making these a part of your life, you have a good start on the spiritual stability you will need to hold up under the stress of your husband's crisis.

Two important keys necessary for strength during this trying time are preparation and endurance. You prepare spiritually for your husband's crisis by having your own spiritual life in order and by doing those things that keep you in fellowship with the Lord and keep you growing. You allow God to bathe you with a sense of his love and care for you personally so that you are strong in the knowledge that you are important to his purpose.

And then you "endure until the end." Some days you will think you are at the end—the end of your wits, the end of your strength. But I mean the end of your husband's crisis. You may literally need to picture yourself doing what the slogan says: "When you are at the end of your rope, tie a knot and hang on!" You will need to make a fresh start each day. In fact, if you're like I was and your husband is like mine during his crisis, you will need many fresh starts throughout the day!

You will need to memorize and practice the following verse: "And let us not get tired of doing what is right, for after a while we will reap a harvest of blessing if we don't get discouraged and give up" (Gal. 6: 9).

You may also find 2 Corinthians 1: 3, 4 a help: "What a wonderful God we have—he is the Father of our Lord Jesus Christ, the source of every mercy, and the one who so wonderfully comforts and strengthens us in our hardships and trials. And why does he do this? So that when others are troubled, needing our sympathy and encouragement, we can pass on to them this same help and comfort God has given us."

11
STRENGTH, STABILITY, AND SANITY

A woman whose husband is old enough to be experiencing his mid-life crisis should have lived long enough to have things fairly well put together in her emotional life. Often, however, that is not the case. She may never have sorted out who she is, discovered what her weaknesses and strengths are, or learned to control her emotions. Or she may have been fairly stable earlier in her life, but because of the chemical changes in her body that signal impending menopause, or because of the unusual stress her husband's crisis has produced, she may now be unraveling emotionally.

HORMONE HOLDOUT

Women who are normally stable, many studies show, can

120

suffer very real emotional problems due to the estrogen deprivation that is associated with menopause. It is sometimes hard to find a physician who will agree, because many men, even highly trained gynecologists, for some reason ignore the estrogen factor and blame other causes. Their attitude only compounds the depressed woman's problems. They imply that it is "all in her head" or that she is not capably handling her personal problems.

Dr. James Dobson, a psychologist and experienced marriage and family counselor, reports that he repeatedly detects the same pattern of emotional symptoms in women who are experiencing their climacteric. He notes that his findings have been verified by Dr. David Hernandez and Dr. Herbert Kupperman, professor of obstetrics and gynecology at New York University.[1] Dr. Dobson strongly advocates the use of estrogen therapy but warns that it is not a "miracle drug" for all the emotional problems of mid-life women. His experience, however, shows that many women who are absolutely miserable and unable to function normally are greatly helped by the appropriate use of estrogen therapy. He suggests that a woman experiencing menopausal disruption of her emotional stability look for a doctor who will treat her correctly, since many doctors still "are grossly uninformed on the relationship between estrogen levels and emotional stability in women."[2]

Dr. Joyce Brothers also decries the hesitancy of physicians to recommend estrogen therapy to suffering menopausal women. She is the wife of a medical doctor and suggests that many doctors have not caught up with the fact that "most women today can expect to live twice as long as women a hundred years ago, [and] medical treatment must change to cope with the challenges of the new female longevity."[3]

Dr. Brothers points out, though, that estrogen therapy is not a fountain of youth. Women with histories of cysts or tumors need careful monitoring. Hormone therapy does, however, slow aging and alleviate many degenerative changes such as the loss of calcium from the bones and loss of muscle tone and substance (which may even be misdiagnosed as arthritis). Loss of skin elasticity, which causes wrinkles, can be postponed. Estrogen also seems to afford protection against heart attacks.[4] All of this in addition to stabilizing the emotions! Dr. Brothers calls menopause the "treatable disease" and declares that on the basis of medical knowledge "there is no reason for most women not to take advantage of [hormone therapy]."[5]

Some of your emotional problems could be due to the chemical changes caused by menopause. If so, they can be easily treated. Let's recognize, however, that your husband's erratic behavior can set off emotional reactions in you that have nothing to do with your estrogen level (except that your hormone level does vary each month—you are emotionally weakest at the time of menstruation because your estrogen level is lowest then).[6] We also need to acknowledge that other physical factors, such as proper diet, exercise, and rest, affect your emotions.

I'M OK

In addition to taking care of the physical causes of your emotional problems, you can take other steps to aid your emotional health. The first is to develop a high self-esteem. A high self-esteem comes from a good self-image. You form your self-image by how well you know yourself and accept all that you are.

Many of us have been taught that high self-esteem or

thinking well of ourselves is a form of pride. We have mistakenly thought that "putting ourselves down" eradicates pride. The truth is that false humility can be a form of pride. We pride ourselves on our humility! Dr. Archibald Hart in *Feeling Free* says that true humility is "characterized by an accurate self-appraisal of both strengths and weaknesses—and a willingness to accept inadequacies."[7]

Gladys Hunt quotes Phillips Brooks on humility: "The true way to be humble is not to stoop until you are smaller than yourself, but to stand at your real height against some higher nature that will show you what the real smallness of your greatness is."[8] Of course, that "higher nature"—the true standard—is Christ. When we compare ourselves to him, we know the "real smallness of our greatness." However, it is also through Christ that we have the ability to be somebody worth something. When we give God the credit for who we are and what we do, we are exercising true humility.

Thinking well of ourselves brings more glory to God, in whose image we are made, than does belittling ourselves. Loving yourself does not mean exaggerating who you are and what your abilities are. Self-love *does* mean that you have made a proper evaluation of your strengths and weaknesses and that you accept yourself as you are *at this time.* You acknowledge God as the source of your strengths, and by his grace and power you are working on any weaknesses that are correctable. Yes, you have a sinful nature and often fall short of God's standard for you, but you can accept his forgiveness and provision for abundant living through Jesus Christ.

Loving yourself means you value who you are, emotionally, spiritually, and physically. You may have what you consider to be physical defects. Some, such as your weight, can be changed. Others, such as the shape of your nose, are less easily changed. You need to accept the unchangeable and realize that God made you the way you are. If you have accepted Christ as your Savior, your body is the dwelling place of the Holy Spirit. Christ died for you and God the Holy Spirit lives within you—you *are* a valuable person!

YOU'RE OK

Jesus assumed we are to love ourselves when he gave the command that we are to love others. He said, "You must love others as much as yourself " (Mark 12:31). A few years ago I suddenly realized that most of the time I wouldn't be loving others very much if I loved them in the same proportion as I loved myself. I have found since then that by accepting and loving myself I am free to accept and love others. In fact, when I become aware that I have slipped back into picking at others, I find that I have started being critical and hard with myself again for some reason. Then I must check what I'm kicking myself about, change it if possible and forgive myself, or accept it if it's unchangeable.

When I am secure about who I am, I can much more easily tolerate the faults and weaknesses of others. When I love and value myself, I love and value others. I am also more at ease around those who might be a threat to me, especially if I view them as prettier, smarter, sweeter, or more capable. Appropriately loving yourself is a very freeing experience. You can enjoy so many more people so much more because you are secure about your own worth. Your energies can be used for constructive activities rather than competing, criticizing, and backbiting. You also don't have to get worn out trying to remake people. When you accept them as they are, they will be more apt to accept you as you are. You also won't be under such pressure to impress others or to defend the way you are.

THE GOOD WHOLE YOU

Hopefully, you and your husband have been building each other's self-image all through your marriage by compliments, appreciation, unconditional acceptance, and accurate feedback on strengths and weaknesses. Many of you, however, may not have been doing these building things for each other, so you may have some deficits in your self-worth now when your husband is less able to contribute to you emotionally. For now, you may need to do your self-appraising and building alone or with a close woman friend. You *need* to build your self-image so that you are as emotionally strong as possible during your husband's crisis. This time will probably be one of the most demanding periods in your life. You will also be better able to help your husband if you have a secure self-esteem.

Dr. Hart suggests three basic steps for the development of a healthy self-image from which self-esteem emerges:

1. Accept God's unconditional love— "Our basic worth must be founded outside of our human potential (or lack of it), and God in His redemptive work on the Cross and His subsequent call to all men to receive His salvation provides the essential basis for our worth."[9]
2. Develop a realistic self-knowledge— " 'Think your way to a sober estimate' (See Romans 12:3, NEB). . . . You must develop a realistic awareness of who and what you are, and this is where pride differs from high self-esteem. . . . pride is characterized by *unrealistic* self-knowledge."[10] An insightful friend can help you get an accurate picture of yourself by lovingly

providing honest feedback.

3. Completely accept yourself: this must be done by yourself— "Thinking one's way through to a 'sober estimate' involves more than just giving intellectual assent to a set of positive and negative qualities about yourself. . . . Whether it is something you are dissatisfied with and can change—or whether it is something that is fixed and unchangeable—you must begin at the same point: *complete self-acceptance.* . . . I am not advocating that you be resigned to your inadequacies. . . . This is simply a step in which you realistically recognize where you are *now.*"[11]

You may realize that you are an impatient person. You need to completely accept yourself as that kind of person at this time. There are some advantages to having a nature that wants to get things done quickly. Your concern, however, is to eliminate the negative aspects of an impatient disposition. Completely accepting yourself as you are sets you free to begin to work toward change so that sometime in the future you will not categorize yourself as an impatient person any longer.

There's no bigger boost to your self-image than to realize that God accepts you for what you are right now. When you fail and when you are inadequate, he provides the forgiveness you need. He is also the enabler who changes you and keeps you growing. Christianity isn't a crutch for the weak. It is life and wholeness! When we appropriate what God has provided for us by a relationship with him, we find we have power, love, and self-control (see 2 Tim. 1:7, RSV)!

MAD IS BAD

In addition to building a strong self-esteem, you will need to learn how to control your anger during this crisis time.

If you've already learned how to do this, so much the better! Many of us, however, have wrestled with our anger most of our lives. As I said earlier, we have been taught that anger is sin. Anger is only an emotion, and is not sin. What we do with anger can become sin.

If you've thought anger was sin, you may have tried to get rid of it by ignoring or suppressing it. Now you find that you feel hostile to almost everyone much of the time or that you are unexplainably depressed. Suppressed anger can also erupt in physical problems such as ulcers and skin disorders.

Perhaps you have joined the school of thought that says you need to vent your anger and express it in whatever way you feel at the moment. You may find, however, that a lot of your relationships with others are disrupted and you do some rash things you later regret. A lot of us are in the middle. We don't regularly suppress our anger, but we don't usually give full vent to it. We feel angry, usually blame someone else, maybe say a few cross things to them, or grump and stomp around awhile until our anger wears off. When we think about the incident in calmer moments later, we feel guilty and perhaps even depressed. We may do this so frequently that we are miserable most of the time.

Hart's *Feeling Free* and Warner's *Feeling Good About Feeling Bad* contain detailed explanations about anger and tell how to effectively control it. Let me share Dr. Hart's suggestions about the steps you should take to deal with anger:

1. Recognize your anger. . . . Pray for sensitivity and self-honesty. Contract with a friend, your spouse, or a parent to tell you every time he or she perceives you as being angry. . . .
2. Release vindictiveness. . . . It is a law of our lower nature that we want to hurt back when we are hurt. . . . *Forgive-*

ness is the key . . . and . . . forgiveness of others is made possible through God's forgiveness of us.
3. Express the anger. . . . [and follow these rules]:
    Try to deal with your hurts and anger as they arise, one at a time. . . .
    Accept responsibility for your anger. It is *your* feeling. . . .
    State your hurt objectively. . . .
    Acknowledge the right of the other person to feelings also. . . .
    Listen, receive, and accept any explanation or apology that may be offered. . . . but do not try to force an apology out of the other person. . . .
4. Make a goal of trying to get understanding between the two of you, and not necessarily agreement.[12]

DANGER AHEAD

To deal with the anger in your life, you should evaluate what kinds of situations most often upset you and lead to your getting angry. Then you should try to avoid those situations or prepare yourself ahead of time if they can't be avoided.

When all three of our daughters were very young, ranging in age from six years to a few months, I found that I was getting angry with them at bath and bedtime nearly every evening. I would scold at them and get impatient with their dawdling ways. Later I would feel guilty for being unloving to them and vow to do better the next night.

My husband helped me think through the causes for my anger and work for solutions. We realized that by the end of a busy day I was exhausted physically and drained emotionally. The girls might still be very active and wound up, but they, too, were getting tired. Our ability to be courteous and kind to each other was wearing thin.

Once someone started with a negative attitude, it was easy for everyone to join in or to retaliate.

As I remember it, I also usually had some of the day's work left over that I was trying to finish—diapers to fold, clean clothes to put away, dessert to make for the committee that was going to meet in our living room later in the evening, and so on. I not only felt tired but I was tense about getting the rest of my work finished.

Jim suggested that I get a short nap during the afternoon while the little ones slept. Then I would be fresher for the evening activities—preparing and serving dinner, cleaning up the kitchen, and getting the girls into bed.

We agreed that Jim would help with the girls when he was home and sometimes take over completely. If he was not involved with the bedtime procedures and was doing something that could be interrupted, I was to call for him as soon as I felt myself getting angry or upset. Knowing I had a way out was a release in itself. After I changed the pattern of events that caused my anger, I was able to avoid the angry feelings and the usual bad actions they produced.

HUMANS WILL BE HUMAN

Anger often comes from frustrated expectations. We need to be less rigid in what we demand of others and ourselves, and we will avoid some of the occasions for anger. Anger also comes from an unforgiving spirit. I see that a lot of my anger is because I expect people to be perfect. When they're not, I hold it against them. Imagine being angry because another person is human!

There are a lot of people going around with grudges they've carried for years. Instead of forgiving the people who have offended them and relinquishing their problems to God to care for, they pile up grievances in their hearts and become sourpusses. I wonder if learning to forgive isn't what makes the difference between a woman who is difficult to be around and one who is a delight.

Ephesians 4:26 is the classic sentence on anger: "If you are angry, do not let anger lead you into sin; do not let sunset find you still nursing it...." (NEB). And the Living Bible gives still more insight, "If you are angry, don't sin by nursing your grudge. Don't let the sun go down with you still angry—get over it quickly; ..." The sentence concludes, "for when you are angry you give a mighty foothold to the devil."

This Scripture seems to assume that people will get angry. But it cautions that anger is dangerous because it gives Satan a good chance to trip us up. We are much more apt to fall into sin when we are angry. One way anger becomes sin is when it is nursed and becomes a grudge.

Wives of men in a mid-life crisis seem to get into more trouble with anger than any other emotion. Eleanor vowed again and again that she wasn't going to get upset when Dan sat around dejectedly staring out the window instead of getting work done around the house. But she would see another Saturday slipping by without needed repair jobs getting done and the yard still looking unkept, and she would be grinding inside!

After several unsuccessful hints or nudges intended to help him get moving, her anger would finally explode. She'd scream something like, "Why can't you do your share around here? All you do is sit and feel sorry for yourself!"

But that wouldn't get him to work either, and finally one day he retorted, "If I can't have peace around my own house, I'll go somewhere else!"

He left in the car and didn't come back for several hours. That incident scared Eleanor enough to start handling her anger in a better way.

AMNESTY

During your husband's mid-life era, you will probably have many reasons to be angry. Recognize the feeling in yourself, look for suitable ways to express your anger, and forgive your husband as quickly as possible. If he is irritable, withdrawn, or gone, you will not be able to talk it over with him. Then you need to imagine that you are face to face with your best friend Jesus and objectively tell him about your hurt as you would if you could talk to your husband. You will need to forgive your husband silently. If he doesn't know he has hurt and angered you and you say to him, "I forgive you," you may start a quarrel. When you are in a touchy situation and communication is inappropriate at the time, all you need to do is have an internal attitude of forgiveness.

You can help avoid feelings of anger by reminding yourself several times a day, "My husband is going through a difficult time right now. I am going to try to understand him and help him. He has had to put up with me through some of my hard times in the past and he may need to help me through some more in the future. I'm the strong one right now, so it's my turn to help him. Because I'm not perfect and God has forgiven me, I can forgive my husband for not being perfect."

Then pray specifically for the Lord to control your thoughts, your feelings, your tongue, your actions, and your reactions.

ABANDONED OR SHACKLED

Another aspect of your emotional life that you may need to work on is your sense of independence or of dependence. By mid-life some wives have become very independent of their husbands, emotionally and perhaps financially. Other wives start out dependent and stay that way. Either extreme can isolate you from your husband during his mid-life crisis.

If you are too independent, he may feel you don't really need him. You may have developed such a separate life-style that you will have little in common with each other. If, on the other hand, you are too dependent, he will probably resent you as a burden he is weary of carrying and try to withdraw from you.

If you have an independent nature and life-style, you don't have to give up your individuality and become a clinging vine. You need to work at being *interdependent,* so you can be a help to him and yet he can feel you need him. You need to hold several conversations with each other to discover what you each need from the other and what you each can contribute to the other. You know best what compromises will work in the light of your particular personalities, careers, values, daily schedule, and the ages of children. You may not need to make external changes so much as changes in attitude.

INDEPENDENCE IN EXCESS

Naomi has always been a very competent, optimistic, and strong woman. Although she gave up a college education to help her husband through his undergraduate and graduate schooling, she is highly intelligent and is a knowledgeable conversationalist on many subjects. Her husband, Bert, is intelligent, too, and has succeeded very well in his career. She is a vibrant, cheerful Christian who bubbles with sunshine and energy. She is one of those women who can competently and apparently effortlessly care for house, husband, children, and guests.

After her children were older, however, she needed more of a challenge and began to work outside her home again. Naomi enjoyed the additional stimulation her career brought to her life. She was well respected and was soon given positions of higher authority at work. The additional finances gave her the freedom to buy things for herself and the family that they could not have afforded on one salary, though that was not the main reason for her working.

Although Naomi cared well for her household, she naturally had less time for some things. One of those was casual conversation with Bert. Quite often, it is the wife who most yearns for time to talk, but in this case Naomi didn't miss it. When Bert began to struggle with his mid-life concerns, he felt he was in the battle alone. His wife neither took his problem seriously nor seemed to want to understand. Because she was finding fulfillment in her career, she didn't notice that Bert was withdrawing. She didn't know how desperately he wanted her to need him in some areas of her life. He spent hours in introspection and his self-esteem was sagging. He felt his wife neither needed nor noticed him, so his self-evaluation always ended with a deficit on his side of the ledger. Consequently, he experienced a deep depression.

Now you think I'm going to tell you he began to have an affair or ran off with another woman. No, he didn't. But he did go through far more lonely agony than he would have if his wife had been more tuned in to him.

Wives don't have to work outside the home to be insensitive to their husbands, however. They can be home being Suzy Homemaker all day and still be thoughtless and incommunicative. Or they can be busy running the primary department in their church's Sunday school, coordinating telephone prayer lines, or planning the P.T.A. carnival.

Does this mean you should never work outside your

home or take on a church, school, or community project? No. But you should prayerfully evaluate your priorities. You might then decide God wants you to eliminate some activities. You might also decide you don't need to drop anything. All you may need to change is your independent, indifferent attitude toward your husband.

THE CLUTCH CRUTCH

At the other extreme is Lena the Leaner. We have mentioned that her husband enjoyed her being dependent upon him when they were first married. But now he is tired of the load and resents her clinginess. When John tries to loosen her clutches, she gets scared and grabs tighter. That makes him resist her more. And on goes the vicious cycle until one of them breaks it.

You may say, "But God says I am the weaker vessel and my husband is to care for me. First of all, the King James Version of the 1 Peter 3:7 passage that says husbands are to "dwell with them [their wives] according to knowledge, giving honour unto the wife, as unto the weaker vessel, ..." doesn't mean that wives are helpless. Bible scholars do not agree on exactly what is meant by the word "weaker." Some feel that Paul was referring to a woman's social status at the time he was writing. Although the Christian message and Christ's example show that "there is no difference ... between men and women: you are all one in union with Christ Jesus" (Gal. 3:28, GNB), the Jewish and surrounding cultures had not given women the same social position and rights as men.

Other scholars, among them the ones who produced the Amplified New Testament, feel that God was referring to women as being physically weaker. Women *are* weaker in physical strength than men, but it is also a scientific fact that they live longer and have a greater resistance to disease than men.[13] Other research shows that women are no less intelligent than men, and Galatians 3:28 says that women are not spiritually inferior. In fact, the remainder of 1 Peter 3:7 says men and women are "heirs together of the grace of God." Women also have responsibility in the world as God directed in the Garden of Eden, "Multiply and fill the earth and subdue it; you are masters of the fish and birds and all the animals" (Gen. 1:29). You will notice that God blessed *them* and told *them* to "multiply... fill... subdue...." He called both the man *and the woman* "masters."

RESPONSIBLE INDIVIDUALITY

God's ideal woman as described in Proverbs 31 is not a weak, clinging vine either. She is industrious about her household duties. She shops wisely and judiciously administers her household. This woman is an investor, making a wise purchase of land. She is an organized planner, and she is enterprising. "She is a woman of strength.... When she speaks, her words are wise..." (Prov. 31:25-26). She doesn't sound like a leaner!

If you are a leaner, remember that when the object you're leaning against moves, you fall over! You need to learn to stand up without a prop. That doesn't mean that you turn your back on your husband and walk away from him emotionally. But there is a big difference between your being "one flesh" with your husband and your being embedded in him like a parasitic tick. "Submitting to each other" (Eph. 5:21) doesn't imply mindlessness. If you didn't have a mind or will of your own, there would be nothing to submit.

MOMENT OF TRUTH

That brings us to the matter of assertiveness. When is it

time for a wife to speak up? How should she go about it? Sometimes when I am counseling wives whose husbands are having a rugged mid-life crisis, I think I must sound like a broken record. I so often say, "Be understanding. Be gentle. Keep patient. Meet his needs." Wives ask both my husband and me how long they are supposed to put up with their mate's unusual antics. If you feel you've taken all the emotional and verbal poundings you can stand and you're on the verge of collapse or explosion, what then? Are there any safety valves?

Virginia was getting tense about the way Fred was treating her. If he wasn't sullen and withdrawn while he was around home in the evenings, he was picking and criticizing. He would barely greet her when he came home from work, slump in front of the tv until he was called for dinner, and then begin crabbing.

"You know I don't like tuna casserole. As much money as you spend on groceries, I'd think you could serve something better than tuna and noodles. Besides, the food bill wouldn't have to be so high if Steve didn't drink so much milk. And he doesn't need homogenized milk either. He can drink skim milk like the rest of us."

He would go on until he left the table to watch more tv. Virginia would feel so irritated with him that she would chip the dishes as she angrily cleared the table. The kids would complain to her about how their dad picked at them, and she would apologize and try to smooth things over. All the while her anger was building.

One night when Fred had been cranky about many little things while they were eating, he started complaining again that Virginia was spending too much money.

"That's it!" she screamed and jumped up from the table, knocking over her chair. She stood over Fred, hands on her hips and yelled, "I've had it! You do nothing but crab and criticize! You sulk around here, expect-

136

ing all kinds of attention and giving nothing but cold silence or dirty jabs in return! I want you to know that I'm not going to take it anymore!"

She grabbed her purse and car keys, slammed out the door, and drove off. She sheepishly returned later that night.

Before you erupt like a destructive volcano because of your husband's erratic and hurtful behavior, learn to use safety releases to handle your tensions. God, other friends, and relevant books can be helpful. Then you may feel it is time to confront your husband about one or several concerns.

WAR AND PEACE

There is, however, a difference between assertiveness and aggressiveness. To be assertive means to express your desires or needs in a positive manner. To be aggressive is to speak or act with hostility. Assertiveness includes the idea of being bold but gently confident about the validity of your message. Aggressiveness connotes a domineering selfishness with disregard of the other's rights.

You'd much rather be assertive than aggressive, wouldn't you? To avoid resorting to aggression means you do some thinking ahead during calm moments and make use of some of the safety valves I've mentioned as you feel the pressure mounting.

After you've used the safety releases—after you've talked to God and to a friend or two, after you've read from a relevant book—plan how you're going to talk to your husband. Don't simply announce, "I've gotta talk to you right now!" Tell him calmly that you need to talk to him and set a specific time. Setting a definite time has the advantages of making sure that you do actually get to talk and that you do it at a mutually convenient time. You would be wise to choose a time that is without pressure. Bad times would be just before he leaves for work, while the children are going to be in and out of the room, or during his favorite television program. Try to suggest a time when you will both be relatively rested and when one of you has not just come from another difficult situation, such as a tension-charged meeting.

Give your husband some idea of what you plan to discuss so that he has opportunity to be prepared, too. Be careful to state the subjects simply and objectively so that you don't set up an inflammatory situation from the start. Don't say, "I want to talk to you. You are being selfish and rude to me lately, and you're always lying about why you come home late from work!" It would be better to say, "Would it be possible to talk to you after dinner tonight? I am concerned about some of the changes I've seen in you lately."

If he should press you for more details right then or become defensive over the mention of his changes, stay calm and quietly say, "Let's not talk about it now when there isn't much time, but let's do talk this evening after dinner."

In the meantime, continue to do lots of silent conversing with God. Ask him to guide your thoughts, make your words kind, keep your emotions calm, and be glorified in the entire discussion.

PRODUCTIVE DIALOGUE

When it is time for your talk, be sure to use a soft, calm voice. "A soft answer turns away wrath, but harsh words cause quarrels" (Prov. 15:1). Clearly communicate what you feel you need to talk about. Keep the explanation short and uncluttered with details. Don't give him more than he can chew in his first mouthful. Be specific; don't expect him to read your mind and then be disappointed when he doesn't. Use feeling words such as "I am puzzled," "worried," "scared," "upset," "concerned," and "disappointed." That way you're not blaming and accusing your husband. You are owning that you *feel* certain ways. Those feelings come from what you are perceiving, but you could be mistaken. Even if you are correct about how you perceive a situation, you are not attacking your husband when you say, "I feel . . . ," "I sometimes wonder . . . ," etc.

Start your sentences with "I" instead of "you." For example, instead of saying, "You are neglecting me," say, "I feel rejected and left out." Instead of declaring, "You always lie," try, "I am unsure of what is the truth." In place of saying, "Your fishy behavior makes me insecure," say "I am apprehensive when you come home late."

When people protest that using "I" messages is simply manipulation, I explain that, although at first the method may seem mechanical, it is a way of helping us be courteous at a time when it would be easy to be discourteous. Using a soft, calm voice may seem like manipulation to someone who usually hollers, but speaking gently promotes peace and doesn't make the listener feel he is being "badgered." Using "I" messages as well as a soft voice reduces aggression and selfishness and is worth the practice!

"I HEAR YOU SAYING . . ."

Check occasionally for feedback from your husband. True communication is not taking place if he is not listening or if he is inaccurately receiving what you say. You might ask, "What do you understand me to be saying?" A

139

lot of trouble comes when you are unaware that you aren't being understood. You assume your husband is thinking along with you and will respond as you expect. You need to hear him say what he thinks you said. You may then need to restate and clarify your concerns until he is understanding what you mean.

In return, you need to give him feedback on what he says. You might say, "This is what I think I hear you saying. . . ." You need to be sure you understand what he really means.

You may have asked for the meeting, but don't forget to let your husband talk, too. He may react strongly to what you say, but hear him out. He may try to sidetrack you with extraneous issues. Or he may counterattack by criticizing you. Acknowledge the issues he brings up, but gently guide the conversation back to the main topic. Perhaps you can tackle the other issues later.

There are some *don'ts* for your dialogue:

- *Don't* present your opinions as facts.
- *Don't* say "always" and "never"; they indicate that you are exaggerating.
- *Don't* be haughty or sarcastic in your attempt to be assertive.
- *Don't* be dishonest; you want him to be honest.
- *Don't* forget to pray for God's help in your conversation, in your decisions, and in carrying them out.

DOCILE DOORMAT

You may decide that being a doormat to your husband will be easier than trying to confront him assertively with your concerns. The problem is that most doormats break after a while and sometimes do something rash that could have been prevented if they had tried to work things out courteously earlier. Even if the doormat is content to remain a doormat, she is denying the true person God meant her to be. She is sinning by not using the talents and opportunities God is giving her. Dennis Gibson, a psychologist and marriage and family counselor, and his wife, Ruth, in an article, "Speaking Up to Your Husband," say, "A doormat wife does not show respect for her husband. Her godly duty is to call forth Christlike actions and attitudes on his part. The wife who suffers silently disobeys God. She does not give her husband an opportunity to be Christ to her. She does not clearly alert him to her needs."[14]

David Augsburger, in *Caring Enough to Confront,* tells us, "Conflict is natural, normal, neutral, and sometimes even delightful. It can turn into painful or disastrous ends, but it doesn't need to. Conflict is neither good nor bad, right nor wrong. Conflict simply is. How we view, approach, and work through our differences does—to a large extent—determine our whole life pattern."[15] Augsburger then shows that "speaking the truth in love" is Christ's example of mature relationships and is the caring-confronting way of responding and respecting each other. His book would be a good one for you to read if you struggle with the extremes of being a doormat or being too aggressive. You can see that a doormat wife shows that she seems not to care enough about her husband to speak the truth in love.

I like what James Kilgore says: "The assertive person believes in his own rights and responsibilities but does not need to blame, dominate, or manipulate his spouse."[16] He also says, "Assertive behavior . . . gives expression to action, demonstrates strength, uses personal skills, accepts responsibility, channels energy positively, and respects the life-space of those involved."[17]

141

MID-LIFE IS A JOKE

Another emotional quality that will be an asset in your life at this time is a sense of humor.

You may say, "There's nothing to laugh at during my husband's mid-life crisis. I don't think it's funny at all!"

True, the crisis itself is difficult but there are times when a sense of humor just might save your sanity. Appropriate humor can lighten the atmosphere for both of you occasionally. A well-timed pun might be one form of humor, or another would be the use of old family "inside" jokes. The old family joke may also remind your husband of the history he has with you and the children at a time when he may be weighing whether there is value in remaining in the family. One of the most valuable forms of humor is the ability to laugh at yourself. When you are apt to be under a strain much of the time, you can provide relief for yourself and those around you if you laugh at the blunders you make.

You can imagine how I latched onto this statement from a recent *Family Weekly* article, when I first read it:

> State University of New York studies of the practical uses of wit and humor show that joking provides a very useful channel for covert communication on touchy subjects which might not otherwise be broached without jeopardizing a relationship. Often, a . . . situation may be so loaded with intangibles as to be potentially explosive. (Sound like anything you've experienced lately?) . . . communication exploring such situations in depth may often be safely carried out by well-placed jokes, . . . purposeful kidding and the like. . . . judicious use of humor can enable us to traverse with immunity over otherwise hazardous areas.[18]

THE HUMOR BOND

During this time when you and your husband may feel

you have little in common, it might help to know that humor can create a bond between you. Jacob Levine says, "Heartily laughing at the same thing forms an immediate bond between people, much as enthusiasm for the same ideals does."[19] Maybe humor is part of the way back to a closer relationship with your husband.

Do you feel you are too old to laugh? Research at the University of Southern California shows that "a sense of humor develops and grows during a lifetime as we become more mature and better able to see the funny side of life's foibles and laugh at our own. One of the evidences of emotional maturity is the ability to see something funny in a difficult situation."[20]

AND THEN . . .

Some other suggestions for keeping your emotional stability during your husband's mid-life crisis are:

- Live one day at a time. In fact, you may need to measure time by moments rather than days or hours.
- Cultivate a positive, cheerful attitude.
- Don't be a martyr or a stoic. Be genuine.
- At the same time, be strong. Allow yourself to cry, but not in front of your husband. (My husband let me know that my crying would only increase his guilt and he felt powerless to remedy the situation. He knew me well enough to know that often in the past I would break down and cry when I felt hurt or unhappy. He saw my swimming eyes, as I forced back my tears, but he didn't have the strength to help.)
- Remember the good times you've had together. It's easy to think that things have always been bad, but recall your memories of happy times.

- "Keep your eyes on Jesus, our leader and instructor. . . . If you want to keep from becoming fainthearted and weary, think about his patience . . ." (Heb. 12:2, 3).

We've been considering the internal parts of you—your spiritual and emotional life—now let's look at the more external aspects—your social and physical life.

12
THE FRIENDSHIP CONNECTION

In our research of mid-life women, Jim and I asked how friends had been a help to them or how they could have been a better help. The responses fell into the following categories:

Friends were most helpful who
- were understanding
- didn't belittle the situation
- had a big listening ear
- kept the couple's problem confidential
- offered unconditional acceptance
- did not have negative personalities
- promoted positive, upbuilding attitudes
- kept in frequent contact
- had also had marital or similar troubles so they were more understanding

- kept the children occasionally so the couple could have time alone together
- included their entire family in some activities

If the husband had left the home, it was helpful if friends complimented the wife on what she was doing well in handling the children alone, and if they invited her and the children to activities. It was important for other men to spend time with her sons to provide some male modeling for them.

WHERE ARE THE FRIENDS?

During trouble of any kind, friends can help you make it through until things level off again. As you can see, however, when troubles involve family relationships, you need to have those friendships established beforehand. People usually rush to the aid of victims and show all sorts of kindness when there is death, sickness, injury, or calamity such as fire, flood, or tornado. However, if you and your mate are having extreme interpersonal stress, there is not usually such a rush of friendship. In fact, many people you might have counted on as friends seem to grow cold and distant when news of your problem gets around.

This coldness on the part of your friends probably is not so much because they no longer want you for a friend as that they do not know what to say or how to act. I speak from experience. Many times I have been tongue-tied when I've seen a friend at church, in the store, or at a party who is in the process of a divorce or some similar trauma.

I remember seeing Beth walk slowly away from the church every Sunday. I knew she was in agony about her husband living with another woman. I often answered the phone when she would call in tears to talk to my husband who was counseling her and trying to bring about a reconciliation. She knew I was aware of some of the problem, but I didn't know what to say when I saw her on Sundays. I wanted to let her know that I cared, but somehow I was so afraid I'd offend her that I ended up saying little, if anything, meaningful.

If a person has talked some to me about her problem, I have more grounds for a conversation. But some troubled people aren't brave enough to bring up their problems. And they shouldn't have to be the initiators in such a case. They are the ones who hurt; I should be the one who helps.

I mention these matters so that you will understand if your friends seem hesitant to talk to you. They probably want to, but they haven't had any practice talking to people with mid-life problems.

Sometimes I don't say much to troubled people because I don't know how much of their problem I'm supposed to know. If they confided in someone, their hurt would be increased if they found out that others knew more than they should. Perhaps your friends have this problem, too.

HELPING THEM HELP YOU

Our daughter Becki is an amputee due to bone cancer. As soon as friends started coming to see her in the hospital after her surgery, she learned that she was the one who had to put them at ease. They would stand by her bed, avoid looking at the empty space on the bed where her left leg should have been, and talk very little.

Becki joked, "Want to know how I lost fifteen pounds in three hours?" Or "Wanna see my new basketball?" (The end of her limb was swollen and bandaged to the size of a basketball.) She named her prosthesis "Harold

147

the Hairless Wonder" and says, "Just think how much money I'll save on razor blades the rest of my life!" When she meets someone new, she usually brings up the subject of her missing leg or her obviously artificial leg so the new friend won't feel embarrassed and will know she can talk about it with her. Unfortunately, interpersonal stress with a family member may not be so easy to discuss. Try, at least, to let others know if you want to talk about the problem.

Some friends may not want to bring up the subject of a mid-life crisis because they are beginning to see some of the signs in themselves and are trying to avoid thinking about it. Others may already be in the middle of it and may feel that it is shameful and that they have somehow failed spiritually. Remember, most of your peer group are being affected to some degree by this problem.

You need to make friends and get to know them well so that when the crisis hits they will give you the extra support you will need. Quality relationships take time. You usually can't develop them the moment you are in dire need of a friend. You need to be forming friendships with many people all through life. Your goal in making friends is not simply to have them on hand if you should get into trouble, of course. Friends are for the sharing of common interests and being available to help one another. As you each unselfishly enrich the other's life, you will then be able to minister to each other when needs arise.

I had two special friends, Roberta and Eileen, who knew a little of what was going on during Jim's mid-life crisis. Each of their husbands had also gone through recent upheavals, and Jim and I had been involved in helping them make it through their difficulties. These two women kept in frequent touch with me by telephone. I didn't have to give them details. I could talk as much or as little as I wanted. They kept me encouraged and helped me keep a balanced perspective. I knew they were earnestly supporting Jim and me in prayer and that they weren't telling other people about Jim's struggles.

INPUT AND OUTPUT

There are three types of relationships that we all need in our lives. One is when a person ministers to you and you do not necessarily ever do anything in return to help that person. God is in this category. So may be your pastor, a counselor, or some other person who is spiritually more mature than you. The second form of friendship is the peer relationship. You and another person share, build, and minister to each other in a give-and-take association. The third kind of friendship is—you guessed it!—the one in which you minister to someone else and perhaps never receive anything in return. In some instances, your children are in this category, along with spiritually weak or otherwise needy folks to whom you minister.

We each need all three kinds of friendships in our lives. Our reservoir of emotional and spiritual strength will run dry if we don't have someone who ministers to us. We need God to be filling us, as well as some other human helpers giving input. The give-and-take peer relationship is also necessary for our growth and development as whole persons. If we have no outlet to others, we grow stagnant. We need to be pouring out what we have and know into someone else's life who is coming along behind us. I have noticed that when I begin to feel lonely and isolated, it is often because I am neglecting one or more of these relationship areas. We need some of each kind of friendship to keep us balanced. If we major in one or two and neglect the others, we will be lopsided.

I've mentioned that during Jim's mid-life upheaval I drew heavily on God's friendship to minister to me through each day. I also had Roberta and Eileen with whom I had the give-and-take peer relationship. Events had happened eariler in their lives and I had been a strength to them. But during Jim's worst year, these two friends had to bolster me and I did little for them in return. They were a very real help to me.

I also realized that I needed to be doing something for someone else. Yes, I was doing a lot for Jim, but that was to be expected. Right then I wasn't teaching any Bible studies or Sunday morning classes. So I decided to start an informal process of building in the lives of some young, single career women. Sometimes we went out to lunch together, other times one or two of them would come to my home to talk to me. Often I would chat with them before or after church services. Helping them grow spiritually and emotionally as they wrestled through times of career change, dating or lack of dating, apartment mate problems, and so on, was a good outlet for me and added fulfillment to my life.

During this difficult mid-life time, you will need all three kinds of friendship. It is not easy, however, to minister to others when you are feeling threatened and anxious. If you can muster even the smallest amount of emotional strength to help someone else spiritually or in other ways, you will find this act to be therapeutic.

There are always people to whom we could be ministering. There are lonely, elderly people who need a visit, a ride to the grocery store, or a light bulb changed. Some handicapped folks could use the same helps. Some young mothers would be glad if someone occasionally took their kids for a couple hours so they could do something for themselves. The church secretary can often use a volunteer for stuffing envelopes or collating booklets. The list is endless. You can make one that applies to your world.

You may reject God's offer of friendship because you feel he has not been coming through for you. If he were a true friend, you think, he would change this situation quickly. When you begin to feel this way, you need to read such Scripture sections as Ephesians 1 and some of the Psalms that assure you of God's love and concern, even if the circumstances at the present are not the way you would like them. You might find other Christian reading helpful. I would suggest *Love Is Now,*[1] *When There Is No Miracle,*[2] and *Where Is God When It Hurts?*[3].

PEER SUPPORT

Developing and maintaining good peer friendships is also important. You are wise if you have many of these going before your husband's crisis hits. You naturally will have some friendships that are deeper than others. You need a few close friends with whom you can share your whole heart and who will be available to hold you up when the situation gets desperate. You may have others who also know of your problem and will be praying for you and your husband, but who don't know all the details. You don't have the emotional energy to share deeply with everyone, and not everyone has *you* as her best friend.

Let me remind you again to keep only women as your close, sharing friends so that you will be able to relate deeply without becoming sexually involved. The exception would be your pastor or a counselor who is trained as a professional. Your sorrows and confusion will be multiplied if you seek help from a male friend and the two of you become romantically interested in each other. You are at a vulnerable time when your husband is not meeting many of your needs. Be wise ahead of time and share your heart only with women or with your counselor.

GROWING A FRIEND

You know that to have a friend, you must be a friend. You can't expect to receive attention, kindness, and help if you never give any. If you have sown the ingredients for friendship, you will reap friendship. If you have been too occupied, selfish, or thoughtless to care for others, don't expect caring people to come out of the woodwork when you have a need. It's never too late to start building friendships, though. If you have a shortage of friends, begin now to develop one or two in depth. Keep your motives straight, however. Don't plan to strike up a relationship solely for the purpose of meeting your needs; a genuine peer friendship occurs when you each unselfishly care for the other.

Who do you choose for a friend? There are many factors, but John Powell lists these: "The amount of things I can share in common with another, our capacity to fulfill each other's needs, temperament, interests, intelligence, values, artistic and athletic abilities, physical appearance, right down to that mysterious thing called 'chemistry.' "[4] As a Christian, some of your closest friends will probably share your faith in Christ. Some of your best friends should be geographically near enough to you so that frequently you can be together face to face. When things are really tough—right after receiving news that your husband wants a divorce or is seeing another woman—it will help if a friend can be with you.

FRIENDSHIP, NOT OWNERSHIP

Remember that your friend isn't your possession. Loy

McGinnis in *The Friendship Factor* reminds us of this fact.[5] Your friend may be your richest treasure on earth at the moment, but don't be jealous if she has other friends. As a mother, you know that when each child was added to your family, you didn't love the others any less—your heart simply expanded with more love. If your friend has other relationships besides the one with you, she doesn't love you less than she would if you were her only friend.

There is another word of caution. Proverbs 25:17 warns, "Don't visit your neighbor too often, or you will outwear your welcome!" You need to be with friends, but you have to use common sense about how much to be with them. Have a clear understanding with them so they can let you know if there are times when they must be doing other things and so you can let them know when you really must have their support.

Georgia had an unhappy marriage, so she found people she could pour out her troubles to. My Christian friends and I felt sorry for her and wanted to do what we could to help. One after another, however, we wearied of her long telephone conversations or personal visits. She was a needy person, but she didn't take her eyes off herself long enough to see that others also had needs.

She lived near Marj and began going every day to her house to talk. She would stay for hours, seemingly not caring that she was greatly inconveniencing Marj's entire family. They would come home in the evening from school and work, have dinner, and go on their individual ways again without any opportunity to be together as a family. Marj could see that the friendship was lopsided and unhealthy and that she wasn't helping Georgia to find any real solutions.

Finally late one afternoon Marj said frankly, "Georgia, I'm sorry, but you've got to go home now. I think that if you'd spend the time and energy doing things for your husband that you spend sitting in my kitchen, I think your marriage would be better. Your long visits are disrupting my family's life. You are welcome to come for an hour or two every once in a while, but I just can't see you all day every day."

Of course, Georgia was offended and never returned. How much better it would have been if she had been sensitive to what she was doing and not have "outworn her welcome." Georgia is an extreme example, but you get the point: Don't be an insensitive pest.

On the other hand, don't let this story keep you from contacting your friends when you need them. Part of the basics in your relationship should include the other's freedom to let you know if she doesn't have time to help you right at the moment. Having more than one friend will give you someone else to turn to if the first friend is unavailable.

"A HELP IN TIME OF NEED"

Lowenthal and Haven have done some exhaustive studies on friendships, their meanings to the people involved, and what people use friends for. One of their conclusions that excited me was, *"having a confidante eases major life adjustments at all ages.* A confidante can support us, validate our beliefs, and act as a 'sounding board' when we need to 'let off steam.' "[6] And that's why it's important for you to have at least one true friend during this crucial time. The proverb says, "A true friend is always loyal, and a [sister] is born to help in time of need" (Prov. 17:17).

FRIEND OR KIN?

Interestingly, Lowenthal and Haven's studies found that

not many relatives were considered close friends. If a woman in her middle years named a relative as a good friend, it was usually a sister. Perhaps this lack of relatives as close friends is because in today's mobile society we seldom live in the same community with our relatives. Perhaps it is also because many family members have not practiced accepting and affirming one another, and they are afraid to let their relatives know when they are having trouble. I also think that women may not share their problems with relatives for fear of hurting them. Your husband is their son or son-in-law, brother or brother-in-law, or nephew. What is causing you grief will grieve them, too. A friend from the outside is more neutral and less vulnerable to the pain.

When Jim was experiencing his mid-life crisis, I did not tell our relatives many details. His parents and mine live in other states, as do our brothers and sisters. After a time, in my weekly letters I did begin to let them know that he was undergoing stress, but I was not very specific about his behavior. I asked them to pray for physical and emotional relief for him. They knew when he came down with infectious mononucleosis and had a hard bout with flu later on, but I could not tell them about some of the strange ways he was thinking and acting. I didn't want to hurt them, and I didn't want them to think poorly of him. I also didn't want them to become alarmed and get involved in our lives with words and actions that would only have complicated things. I felt I didn't have the strength to cope with *their* emotions, too.

Had our relatives lived closer, they would have made their own observations. We would have had more time together, and they wouldn't have had sketchy information. As it was, they were supportive and concerned, even with only partial knowledge. They kept in touch by letter and prayed faithfully. The value of their relationship with us can only be measured when I imagine how it would have been not to have had their love and concern.

FRIENDS CAN COME IN GROUPS

Besides having individuals as friends, you will be most wealthy if you also have a small group of people with whom you are close. The group might meet for Bible study, prayer, deep sharing, a work project, or a hobby. The important thing is that you gather regularly and touch each other's lives in some meaningful way. They may be people with whom you can share your hurts and anxieties over your husband's behavior.

It is riskier to share your problems in a group, though, because you need to know how much you can trust each one. Some will be more affirming than others. You may decide that it isn't appropriate to share with the entire group, but meeting with them is still helpful if what you are doing when you meet is meaningful to you.

Activities with a group provide the stimulation, input, and outlet that you need to keep you from becoming too absorbed with your problems. From the group you may find some of the few close friends you need at times when the group isn't meeting.

Earlier I mentioned Donna who stayed in the denial stage too long when her husband asked for a divorce and who then tried to commit suicide. Donna got into a small Bible study and sharing group in which she received a lot of support from the other members. She could pour out her feelings and fears to them at the meetings and to individuals during the week. Some group members took her and her children with them for family picnics, miniature golfing, and church socials. Their care for her helped her through her rough time of adjustment during and after her divorce.

VULNERABLE LOVE

The key to success in having helpful friendships is in finding people with whom you can be open, honest, and affirming. This means that you are willing to be vulnerable and that they reciprocate by also being vulnerable. For you to continue your openness and honesty, they also need to be open and honest. You affirm and build them, and they support and help you. There will be times when you receive more from them than you give to them, but there will also be times when the process is reversed. Your model for the kind of sacrificial love and acceptance this kind of relationship requires is Jesus Christ. As you study the Gospels, you will be overwhelmed with the unconditional love Jesus has for people.

Christ's unconditional love was so fully expressed in his relationship with that impulsive, uneducated, smelly fisherman Peter—the aspiring water walker who started to sink, that tempter who wanted to thwart Christ's Jerusalem mission, that ear-slashing hero who had fallen asleep while "watching and praying" with Christ, that dogmatic friend who vehemently swore that he didn't even know Christ, that ministry dropout who went back to his old ways when Christ seemed to have left the scene. Christ poured information into him, entrusted him with responsibility, sought him out several times, assured him of his love, and always dealt with him in love. He saw the potential in Peter and was the enabler in developing him into the dynamic, useful servant he became.

In *No Longer Strangers* Bruce Larson says,

> We Christians must begin to realize that in living out the dynamics of the gospel we must become radically vulnerable and radically affirmative to those with whom we live. Certainly this will be costly, and will often fail. But apart from this kind of radical behavior, there is sometimes no way in

which God can work through us to build some deep re-lationships. . . . This radical style of life in Christ has many pains, but anything less has few pleasures. The more we guard our lives and the more we protect ourselves, the more lonely and withdrawn we become. As we discover in Jesus Christ both the example we need and the power to live as He lived, we go through the pain into a life of deep, loving relationships.[7]

The price you pay in relating openly and meaningfully to develop relationships will be more than repaid as you reap the benefits. You will experience personal growth and have someone's help in troubled times, as well as know the joy of enriching someone else's life. As you reach out to add worth and meaning to someone else's life, you will find your own worth and meaning increasing. As you accept your friend's love and in turn love your friend unconditionally, you also begin to experience a tiny bit of how much Christ loves and accepts you. When you see a human friend sacrifice time and emotional energy to meet your needs, you understand a little more about Christ's sacrifice of his life for you.

Quality friendships are invaluable at any time and are especially helpful during the stress and pressures of your husband's mid-life crisis. Quality friendships will also teach you how to be a true friend to your husband at this crucial time.

Other important factors influencing how well you manage during this time are your physical health and appearance, so what can you do about them?

13

OLDER, BUT BETTER!

"You're not getting older you're just getting better,"
They whispered with a grin.
But if I am getting better,
Why do I have to suck my stomach in?

If I'm getting better and not getting older,
Why do they offer me
Dye for my hair, creams for my skin,
And Geritol to boost my energy?

If I'm getting better and not getting older,
Why do I feel morose
When my feet and ankles swell
And I see all my veins are varicose?

> If I'm getting better and not getting older,
> Why do they laugh and jeer
> When I begin to pant and fan
> And ask why it is so hot in here?
>
> Since I'm getting better and not getting older,
> My higher self decides
> To develop inner beauty.
> But, Lord, couldn't I look sexy besides?[1]

Like it or not, we mid-life women are caught in a battle with beauty. It is difficult to balance between spending hours and fortunes trying to maintain or regain our beauty, and giving up completely. We tell ourselves that who we are counts more than how we look. But most of us know that, as Joyce Landorf says, man certainly does look on the outward appearance. And that includes our husbands.[2] We have experienced how much better we feel about ourselves if we feel physically attractive. Our outside influences our inside qualities, and vice versa.

THE ENEMY

We may spend dozens or hundreds of dollars on cosmetics, hairdos, clothes, and even face-lifts, but we have a relentless enemy—age! Some of us are more successful in hiding it than others, but as time marches on, so do the wrinkles and fat rolls! We may diet and exercise until we are red in the face, but our aging progresses relentlessly. We may let up on the dieting and exercising, but aging never lets up.

Women at mid-life, more than at any other time, are highly concerned with their appearance because they equate attractiveness with youthfulness.[3] Since they are no longer youthful, they conclude they must no longer be

160

attractive. And our world places a strong emphasis on being attractive. You must be attractive to win your husband and keep him. You must be attractive if you are working outside your home. You must be attractive if you wish to be respected as you offer your services to the church, community, or school. The pressure is always there, even in Christian circles. It isn't all bad, but you can certainly lose your perspective about what is and isn't important in life.

A lot of the dilemma comes from the stereotype into which our society puts mid-life women. Women with wrinkles and sagging shapes are considered ugly and even repulsive, while mid-life men with gray hair—or no hair at all—and a thickening waistline are often considered "mature" and desirable. This heightens the problem for the mid-life wife whose husband is looking at younger women who also find him attractive. Eventually both the husband and wife will come through this period of time, with her accepting her appearance and his feeling content to be with someone who has aged like he has. But during those midyears, many women live in agony over their physical appearance.

PASSING YOUTH—SAGGING WORTH

According to research, mid-life women judge their worth by their appearance more than women of any other age group. They seem less able to assess their other qualities objectively if they are losing their youthfulness. One researcher noted, "Insofar as women are valued for beauty and female beauty is equated with youth, aging robs a woman of her main value and her self-esteem."[4]

This researcher observes that men are permitted two standards of physical attractiveness—the youth and the man. A man's desirability is enhanced by signs of aging and by his power, wealth, and achievement, which have increased with age. Women are permitted only one standard of attractiveness—beauty associated with youthfulness. So, you can see why it is easy for an aging woman to begin to hate herself. But, have you noticed, "Nobody who survives youth keeps the body of youth"?[5] What are we to do? Give up? Fight harder? What should be the Christian woman's attitude?

INNER LOVELINESS—OUTER UGLINESS

In spite of our culture's pressure for youth and beauty, many people have come to realize there is more to a woman than her exterior. Men may be attracted initially to a pretty, young woman, but if her spirit is ugly and selfish, they lose interest. But some women excuse their overweight bodies, stringy hair, and nondescript faces through the "beautiful soul" syndrome. Why can't beautiful souls come in attractive containers? There is no excuse for packaging the Spirit of God in a shoddy wrapping. You are not necessarily a vain person if you watch your weight, care for your hair and face, and dress attractively.

You may have some "givens" that you don't consider ideal and that can't be easily changed, such as a short chin or closely set eyes. But most of us could do a lot more with what we have than we do. I'm sure right now you can think of women who have unattractive facial features but who have learned to create beauty with makeup and hairstyle. On the other hand, you know ordinary, or even ugly-appearing, women who have good facial features and could be beautiful if they used makeup appropriately and styled their hair. Making the most of your physical appearance is good stewardship, the same as making good use of time or talents.

I think of Esther who used to look drab. Her hair was clean but blah. She wore no makeup because she felt Christian women shouldn't. There was nothing wrong about her clothes—that is, if she'd been wearing them a decade earlier. When she started working part time in an office with other women, she realized that her husband lived all day around attractive women who generally were on their best behavior. She gradually began to change her appearance so that today she is a very appealing woman. Her hair is in a bouncy, attractive style. She wears a moderate amount of makeup which enhances her warm eyes and smile. Her clothes are appropriate and accented with contemporary accessories. The new Esther is also more outgoing and friendly because she feels confident about her appearance.

HUMAN ECOLOGY

God is the creator of beauty. We are all for preserving and appreciating the beauty of nature—woods, grasslands, flowers, sky, rivers and lakes, birds and animals. The human body is also part of God's creation, and it isn't wrong to preserve, groom, and appreciate that part of God's handiwork, too.

Our body is also the temple of the Holy Spirit, if we are God's children. The temple that Solomon built for God, as described in (1 Kings 5: 2—6: 38), was no dumpy hovel built from leftover scraps! The finest materials were used by the most skilled craftsmen. Even the tabernacle, the temporary dwelling place of God while the Israelites were on the move, was carefully and beautifully made from costly materials (Exod. 35: 4—39: 42). It seems appropriate, then, to do as well with God's human dwelling places.

Of course, any good thing can be overdone—or

underdone!—and then become sin. You can spend too much time, thought, and money on your physical appearance. We are warned not to be "concerned about the outward beauty that depends on jewelry, or beautiful clothes, or hair arrangement" (1 Pet. 3:3). The meaning here is not to be *overly concerned* and not to depend on the outward trappings to make real beauty. The Amplified New Testament and New American Standard Bible use the phrase, "*merely* external." Joyce Landorf says she is sure Paul didn't mean we couldn't use any of the externals: "for if we carried out his words to their literal end, they would require that women go nude. 'Whose adorning let it not be that of ... putting on of apparel' "[6] (KJV).

The emphasis is to be on the inner qualities named in the verse that follows: "Be beautiful inside, in your hearts, with the lasting charm of a gentle and quiet spirit which is so precious to God" (1 Pet. 3:4). You can possess the lasting beauty of a gentle and quiet spirit by knowing and reflecting Jesus. If you are plain of face and lacking in figure, you can still be beautiful when your face and attitudes mirror the sweet disposition of Jesus.

FIGHTING THE BATTLE

There *are* some specific things you can do to maintain or regain your physical attractiveness. Almost every daily newspaper and several monthly magazines for women contain hints on diet, exercise, and care for skin and hair. We get so used to seeing these articles and the advertisements for products to help, we almost become immune to their effect. At least, we become so confused we don't know what to do first. So we do nothing.

Your common sense will be of some help to you. Perhaps you can recall that the health books you studied in school stressed that proper diet, rest, fresh air, exercise, and cleanliness were important to health and a healthy appearance. Those would be good places to start.

For definite direction in each of those areas, I have found a good help in Gloria Heidi's *Winning the Age Game.* [7] It contains very easily read, practical information on fashion, makeup techniques, hair care, diet, exercise, poise, menopause, as well as face-lifting and challenges for your sex life. Her hints are the kind that are of lasting help, not faddish. When I first saw there were sections on makeup and fashion, I thought I wouldn't bother to buy the book because trends in those areas change quickly. As I read further, I saw that her advice will still be valid long after fads and trends have changed many times.

WORDS TO THE WISE

Winning the Age Game is fun to read. But don't lose your perspective and become obsessed with being an "ageless woman."

Better Than Ever by Joyce Brothers also has some great beauty hints. She conveys the impression, however, that a woman's main goal in life is to win a sex partner, whether or not he is your husband.

You need to strike a balance between making yourself physically attractive and spiritually vibrant. Keep your feet in the Scriptures and remember that you want your earthly temple to reflect the Lord. On the other hand, don't use spirituality as an excuse for being dumpy and drab. I really appreciate Christian writers such as Joyce Landorf and Anne Ortlund[8] who advocate physical attractiveness and show how to develop true inner, spiritual beauty.

We are going to assume that you are already working on the spiritual and emotional parts of you so that the inner beauty is developing. Let's take a quick look at some areas of your physical appearance you can improve. Perhaps you will get stimulated to do some more serious study and work on your weak areas. That will make you more attractive to your husband—and yourself!

First of all, you need a healthy, rested body. By this time in life, you probably know how many hours of sleep you need each night to feel rested and ready to go in the morning. The number of hours in bed aren't as important as whether you are truly relaxing and getting rebuilt during those hours. If you are having trouble sleeping, try deliberately to give all your cares to the Lord as you are ready to go off to sleep. Let God run the world for you for a few hours. If there are physical reasons why you can't sleep, get help from your physician. A word of caution, however: many medical doctors quickly prescribe sleeping pills that can cause dependency or other ill effects. Try to get your doctor to help you with other remedies before you resort to sleeping pills. Vigorous exercise during the day or early evening, and drinking milk or a warm nonstimulating drink at bedtime may help. You need an adequate amount of sleep to function best during your waking hours. Problems that seem monumental when you are tired are much smaller when you are rested.

Be sure to see a doctor once a year for your Pap smear and for checking any other physical needs you may have. Since cervical cancer is one of the most common forms of cancer among women and yet one of the easiest treated if detected early, it is disrespect for God's temple not to get an annual Pap smear. You are the one to make and keep the appointment. Your children may nag you to get some smarter clothes or change your hairstyle, but not too many check to see if you have had your annual physical.

exam. If you don't know how, ask your doctor to show you and to give you a pamphlet to take home to refer to until you remember how. Or find the information at your library and make a photocopy of it on the copy machine available right there.

BODY CHEMISTRY

At mid-life your physical health and emotional well-being are affected by your diet. What you eat affects not only your weight and figure, but also your energy, emotional resilience, and other aspects of your health. Your need for supplemental vitamins is greatly increased because of the tremendous stress on your body during this time.

If you ask your doctor about vitamins, however, he will probably smile condescendingly and say, "Now, Mrs. Mid-Life, you get all the vitamins you need from a balanced diet." Or, as one doctor told me, "You can spend your money on vitamins if you want to, but it's like pouring sand down a rathole!"

Medical doctors have a history of denying the nutritional approach to physical and emotional health. It seems that until recently the medical profession has not taken time for much research in this area, and they would not accept the results achieved by others.

Fortunately, more medical doctors are now receiving training in nutrition and recognize its tremendous contribution to health. If your doctor isn't one of them, I recommend that you find one who is.

One of the problems of our so-called "balanced diet" is that much of the nutritional value is lost in the processing and cooking, either in our kitchens or before it reaches our homes. Our food isn't doing us the good it should, and our bodies are in greater need at this time. If you

167

read the two chapters in Gloria Heidi's *Winning the Age Game* that deal with nutrition—"Diet Is a Four-Letter Word" and "The Pause That Distresses"—you will be convinced of your body's need for supplemental vitamins and minerals. Other authors who can help you learn about nutrition are Adelle Davis, Carlton Fredericks, and Linda Clark. Their books are available at most bookstores.

Some time ago I was having trouble with water retention. Two doctors gave me diuretics. I found that I felt extremely weak whenever I took those prescriptions, so I ate more food to try to compensate for the energy loss. I still didn't have much pep, so I didn't exercise much. The extra food very quickly accumulated as fat. So now I was heavier from fat *and* extra water! And I still lacked energy.

Finally, a different doctor took a genuine interest in my situation. Instead of handing me another drug prescription, he did a careful analysis of my blood chemistry and the various prescriptions and self-prescribed vitamins I was taking. On that basis he decided what deficiencies I had and what vitamins and minerals I needed to supplement my diet. It was not long before I felt healthier and more energetic than I had in years.

DIVIDENDS FROM EXERCISE

Exercise is also important for your health. You may think that the exercise you get in doing your housework or keeping up with your career is sufficient. Unless you have nearly quit eating, it isn't. Even if your weight is suitable, you need to exercise for more than just burning off calories. You need to condition your body, tone up your muscles, and increase your oxygen processing.

Why do I mention oxygen processing? Oxygen is the key in converting the food you eat into energy. Your energy level is dictated by your body's ability to get and process oxygen. If you have a well-developed oxygen-processing system, you burn your fuel (food) quickly and efficiently to produce energy. This system is made up of efficient lungs, a powerful heart, and a good vascular system. You contribute to their effectiveness by regularly exercising in a way that forces your body to breathe hard—to need and process oxygen rapidly—for ten to fifteen minutes. Exercise that makes you breathe hard over a period of time is called "aerobic" exercise.

You should start into an exercise program gradually, and you should make sure that your doctor approves of any strenuous conditioning program. For help with an exercise program, I suggest a chapter from *Winning the Age Game,* "Thin Isn't Everything." Gloria Heidi also has some workable suggestions for particular trouble spots for mid-life women—bustline, waistline, midriff, upper arms, and so on.

Exercise will also benefit your emotional well-being at this critical time. Frustrations seem to lessen after a long, brisk walk or other vigorous exercise. Aggressive feelings find a safe outlet through physical exertion. Many counselors have found that the mid-life woman's emotional state greatly improves with regular, strenuous exercise.[9] Your improved physical appearance will also help you feel better about yourself and give you more confidence. Being faithful about exercise and diet also contribute to self-approval and that good feeling you get from being self-disciplined.

YOUR MAN'S LOOKING

You might say, "Well, I'm in favor of all those health hints you've mentioned because I believe in doing my part to have a healthy body. But I'm not so sure that fashion, makeup techniques, and hairstyle are important as long as I am focusing on being a godly woman."

But remember, you are a steward of all that God has entrusted to you, and that includes your physical appearance.

An important consideration, especially at mid-life, is how your appearance affects your husband. Since he is going through a giant upheaval as he rethinks his values and commitments, he is probably looking at you with an evaluative eye. How does he think you look? Do you dress to suit him? Are you sexually appealing? What does he like or dislike about your figure?

Perhaps he hasn't told you what he thinks for a long time. But you may have a good idea of what he likes and dislikes in a woman's appearance. It would be appropriate at this time for you to study his tastes. From your past knowledge and present observations, you can probably piece together a pretty complete picture of what appeals to him. When he is in the right mood and when you can be objective, ask him to tell you what he admires most about a woman. Don't be offended if you don't have all the characteristics he mentions, but do what you can to produce them or improve what you have. God wants you to meet your husband's needs in the area of physical attractiveness.

IS DOWDINESS NEXT TO GODLINESS?

You already know that how you dress is one of the keys to your physical appearance. Even if your clothing budget is small, you can capitalize on what is complimentary to you. It is better to have a few things that look good on you than two closets full of inappropriate clothes.

Some Christian women feel that, most of all, they should not follow the current fashions. Somehow wearing clothes that are five to ten years behind style is more godly. The interesting point is that five or ten years ago some people considered *those* clothes "worldly"!

There are some good reasons for wearing current fashions, one of which is to make you look and feel younger. Some people act as if it were more spiritual to look old. In fact, during this time when your husband may be struggling with being attracted to younger women, you are doing your marriage a favor if you look young. That doesn't mean that you try to squeeze into teenage styles two sizes too small for you! But you *can* choose fashionable, young-looking clothes that are appropriate for you. You should avoid looking matronly.

If you are wearing fashionable clothes, you will have more self-confidence and carry yourself with more poise. When you feel better about yourself, you are free to care about others and not be self-centered. This means that you have chosen your clothes with care. Once you have put them on and made sure everything is in place, you can forget yourself. Have you noticed that you are more concerned with yourself when you are wearing something in which you feel dowdy or out of place? You are less free to concentrate on others because you are preoccupied with your appearance.

Wearing fashionable clothing styles lets your husband and others know that you are not behind the times. Being out of date in your physical appearance and in your thinking is associated with being "old" and "dull." Your husband and other people will feel that you are up with the present world if you're keeping current with today's clothing styles.

Of course, it would be poor stewardship to change your entire wardrobe with every passing style fad. There

171

are also some fashions you should avoid if they are not right for your figure. If you choose more classical styles, you will be able to wear them for more years. You might use a basic suit for years, but you can update it with a current blouse, scarf, or jewelry fashion.

TOPPING IT OFF

The hairstyle you choose should not be dictated by fashion unless it is right for you. Many mid-life women latch onto a short hairstyle, whether or not it looks good on them, because it seems easy to maintain.

Gloria Heidi says women should avoid the "menopause bob." The mid-life woman often chooses a short haircut because " hot flashes" and our busy lifestyle make it hard to care for longer, curly hair. Your hairstyle needs to be the most complimentary one for *you*. You don't need to wear your hair according to the latest fad, nor do you want to look as if you're ten years behind current styles.

Most men like long hair on women, but not all do. You should learn which way your husband prefers yours and wear it to please him. At the same time you need to consider your facial shape, body size, hair texture, and so on. Find a hairstylist who will work with you in finding a suitable style. If you don't plan to go to the hairdresser for a shampoo and set each week, have the stylist show you how to do your hair yourself.

EMPHASIZING THE POSITIVE

Long ago I heard the following little poem derisively chanted:

A little bit of powder

And a little bit of paint
Often make a woman
Look like what she ain't!

Do you know people who feel that using makeup is wrong? "If God had meant for you to have bright red lips, he would have made them that way." That same philosophy could be carried so far as to say, "If God had meant for you to have short fingernails, he wouldn't cause them to grow." (I don't even know any Bible verse that supports the practice of keeping my nails trimmed!) Or, how about, "If God had intended for you to wear clothes, he would have had you born covered"?

Of course, using makeup in excess and taking an inordinate amount of time to apply it is wrong, just as anything in excess is wrong. Maximizing your good features and minimizing your poorer ones, however, is a part of good stewardship. If you apply the same principle in the area of your talents, you would do the things that you are most able to do well and not take time doing those for which you are ungifted. For example, it would be a waste of my time to be church pianist. I reached the limit of my musical ability at a low level. I have other abilities, however, and I exercise those.

We don't criticize people for doing what they are most gifted to do. Shouldn't we have the same attitude about our physical assets?

I know a friendly, lively, shapely girl with beautiful hair and a lovely smile. Unfortunately, she has a nose that is too large for the rest of her features. She has learned to add just the right touch of makeup in the right places to give the allusion of having a smaller nose. As a result, she is a beautiful girl. And I don't call that hypocritical—at least, no more so than for the woman who chooses clothing that doesn't accentuate her large hips.

The opposite of no makeup, of course, is too much makeup or poorly applied makeup. I think of Alice. The first time I saw her with her wig askew, her artificial eyelashes slipping, her eyebrows crooked, and her lipstick smeared, I thought, "She must have had to hurry to get dressed this morning. Or maybe the lighting over her mirror was poor." But the next time I saw her she looked the same. Then I thought, "She's doing it for a joke. She wants to see if someone will say something." I wasn't going to be that someone! I saw her several times again. She always looked as if she had just had a fight with a giant propeller that had a dripping paintbrush attached to it. Her appearance distracted me so much that I had trouble seeing what kind of person she might be.

Josephine Lowman, whose nationally syndicated column appears in many daily newspapers, reports that her response from men indicates "they like makeup if they don't know you have it on—or at least if it is natural enough to look real, . . ."[10] The secret is using enough of the right makeup in the right places to make you look like a natural beauty!

THE FEMININE MYSTIQUE

Another asset for beauty that you possess is your femininity. I know, in the drive to get equal rights for women, some have felt that femininity is sexist and a deceitful ploy to keep women as second-class citizens.

I believe in the equality of men and women, but I don't see that accepting my sexuality makes me second-class. We cannot deny that God created two different sexes and that he gave them different physical characteristics The outrage has come when ungodly cultures have treated the two sexes differently. And a further outrage has been committed when, in the name of Christianity, our church

174

fathers (and recently a few mothers) have perpetuated this difference.

BIBLICAL EQUALITY

If you could completely forget what sex you happened to be born and look without any prejudice at the original language of the Bible, you would see that God intends men and women to be equal in position, authority, responsibility, submission, and as heirs together of God's grace. God created both in his image and gave them both authority (Gen. 2:26-28). They both sinned and they both had consequences to pay (Gen. 3). They each have responsibilities to the other as husband and wife (1 Cor. 7:3-5; Eph. 5:21-33). Christ's example in the Gospels is the ultimate in showing that God intended men and women to be equal. And even those tricky passages in the Epistles, such as those in which women are commanded to keep silent in church and not to teach, can be understood when you know that the issue is fidelity to marriage rather than church leadership roles. For a detailed study on a woman's position in God's sight, I suggest you read *Husband-Wife Equality* by Herbert and Fern Miles,[11] *The Apostle Paul & Women in the Church* by Don Williams,[12] and *In Search of God's Ideal Woman* by Dorothy Pape.[13] For nitty-gritty details on the original language, read *Chauvinist or Feminist? Paul's View of Women* by Richard and Joyce Boldrey[14] and *All We're Meant to Be* by Letha Scanzoni and Nancy Hardesty.[15]

The point I want to make is that you should be true to your sexuality. As an overreaction to the exploitation of women, some have tried to extinguish their sex difference by unisex clothing and hairstyles. Being equal doesn't mean that you have to look the same or hold the same jobs. Being equal *does* mean that if you hold the same job you get the same pay. Being true to your sexuality means that you are free to be the feminine person God created. You do not have to compete with males to prove your worth. You are part of God's creative order because you are female; your husband is also part of God's plan because he is male. Sexuality is the very essence of your personhood. Gladys Hunt says, "Sexuality is the way I express who I am to others. In that sense, everything I do is sexual because I am a woman. To be a woman is a total way of existing."[16]

GLAD TO BE FEMININE

Troll, Israel, and Israel note that

> Sexuality is a part of the whole person.... human sexuality is more than procreation and genitalia, more than orgasm, and more than sex hormones. It suggests the capacity for involvement in all of life that relates to the fact of two sexes. ... The human need for intimacy, love, identity, and human interchange is crucial. The intimacies and warmth associated with human sexuality have importance greater than the release of sexual tension. ... As an affirmation of connection to the energy of life, [the expression of sexuality] is a meaningful assertion and commitment to self.[17]

When you accept your sexuality, you are moving toward the acceptance of yourself as a total person. We have said that self-acceptance is a key to a good self-image, and a good self-image is a key to accepting and loving others. When you accept your femininity, you are closer to peace with yourself. Then you are free to provide for your husband's physical and emotional needs. Ingrid Trobisch in *The Joy of Being a Woman* says, "Living and accepting one's own gender is the greatest help which the sexes can give to each other. I cannot accept my partner unless I accept myself. I cannot love my partner unless I love myself."[18] Mrs. Trobisch challenges us to accept the difficult physical aspects of our being female—our menstrual cycle and childbirth—to "live in harmony" with every part of ourselves.

Why all this talk about being feminine in a chapter on physical health and appearance? If you accept your sexuality, you will enjoy being a woman. This will influence how you care for your body and your physical appearance. Looking great and feeling good will help you *and* your husband during this crucial time of mid-life.

Now we want to talk about specific ways in which you can help your husband survive his mid-life crisis.

PART 4
HELPING YOUR HUSBAND

14
WINNING ATTITUDES

Fran was a mid-life woman who suddenly realized her forty-five-year-old husband was doing things that were quite unlike him. As she reflected, she became aware that he had begun behaving strangely on occasions some months earlier, but she had thought little about it at the time. Now she was acutely aware that something was amiss.

Fran's husband, Ray, was a professional man who was very devoted to his family. He was also a Christian and a leader in his church. He was a humble, unselfish person, and people thought highly of him. He had never been a talker, but when he spoke, he was worth listening to.

Now he was often withdrawn, sometimes sullen, and even filled with self-pity around home. In public he made the effort to appear as friendly as before, but the stress of putting on a front when he felt lousy became so difficult that he began to find excuses not to attend the usual church and community functions. He became cross and snappish. He started working more hours and coming home later than he said he would. Finally he began calling to say he wasn't coming home at all some evenings. He wanted to be alone to think.

That's when Fran snapped into reality. But reality stung. She hurt so much that she eventually sought help from her pastor. He helped her see that Ray was in mid-life transition with many things weighing on his mind and causing him terrific pressure. Fran began to read as much as she could about this period in life so that she could understand Ray. Then she did all she could to help him. The two of them had some rough times for many months. Ray even confessed that for the first time in his married life he was seriously considering another woman. She was younger and he had been able to share some of his concerns with her when Fran hadn't seemed to care. He hadn't meant to get so emotionally involved and as yet they weren't sexually involved, though Ray felt he did love the other woman.

Ray made it successfully through his mid-life crisis without leaving Fran and without leaving his profession. Fran stuck with him through thick and thin. They learned to communicate more honestly with each other and to be more alert to each other's needs. Today their marriage is stronger than ever.

When you started to read this story, you might have thought I was talking about you and your husband. Jim and I have heard similar stories from hundreds of mid-life women. The above account is basically about one couple, whose names have been changed, but the situation fits many mid-life couples today.

ENOUGH IS TOO MUCH

Not all stories end so happily, however. Sue and Pete are a typical example. Pete's mid-life trauma also caught Sue off guard. They were both intelligent, friendly Christians. His profession brought him in touch with many interesting people. His wife was also a growing, fascinating, attractive person. But she did not, at all, understand the turmoil he was telling her about. He had always been so sure of himself and his philosophy of life. Why would he be questioning and doubting his beliefs and values now?

Sue kept busy with the children and her part-time career and didn't let Pete's troubles bother her. When he finally told her he was spending time with a young woman, she exploded. That was enough! She told him to leave and not come back until he straightened out! When he continued to be confused for some weeks and was living with the third in a series of women, Sue filed for divorce. She was convinced he had changed permanently. She hastily remarried. She soon realized she had made a poor choice for a second husband, but she was stuck with him now. Then Pete contacted her to say that he seemed to have his head on straight once more and for the past few months had been feeling like himself again. Would there be a chance of restoring their marriage and reuniting the family?

Not all mid-life marriages are saved or broken because of the wife. But she is nevertheless the big factor in whether or not the relationship stands the strain of the husband's mid-life crisis.

MORE THAN SURVIVAL

The early chapters of this book tell you something about

183

a man's mid-life problems. Perhaps you've done some additional reading in *Men in Mid-Life Crisis* or other books I mentioned in the Suggested Reading List at the back of this book. We've considered the problems your husband's trauma causes you and some ways you can be strengthened to survive. This portion of the book is aimed at giving some practical suggestions so you can help your husband survive. Hopefully, you both will be more than merely survivors. I pray that together you will be triumphant winners!

Your attitudes can make or break your husband—perhaps not totally, but at least to a great extent. When you realize your husband is entering his mid-life transition time or if you want to be prepared for the time when he does, you need to decide what attitudes you are going to possess. You need to decide now, and then you need to rededicate yourself each day—perhaps many times each day. And remember, you cannot keep your vows for positive attitudes by your own strength. You wear down, get selfish, and short-sighted. You need Christ's power in you every moment. Apply Philippians 4:13 to your life: "I can do all things through Him who strengthens me" (NASB).

THE COMMITMENT COST

The first attitude you need is one of commitment. You need to commit yourself to your marriage and to your husband as a person. The major question you must ask yourself is, "Do I want to keep this marriage?" Unless you really want to stay in the marriage, you will probably not be able to live with all the stress and sacrifice you will have over the next three to five years. If you are committed to your marriage, you will need to decide to do everything within your power to keep and improve the relationship.

You also need to determine to do everything you can to support, build, and love your husband.

To put this kind of determination to work means that many times you will have to put your own needs and desires aside and zero in on his. This may be the umpteenth time you've done so this week! But by God's strength, you are going to do so again. And again.

You need to commit yourself to the art of understanding your husband. That means you need to specialize in knowing what your husband thinks, feels, values, worries over, and fears about the future. You need to know what pleases him, how he views himself—everything that makes him what he is.

Then you need to commit yourself to accept him just as he is right now and to help him close the gaps he senses in his life. You are not to decide what you think his needs are, but you have to meet the needs *he is feeling.* For example, he may be complaining that he never gets enough leisure time. You might be tempted to point out all the hours he has spent watching television this week (hours that *you* didn't get because you were busy with the children and the house!). But what he needs is your understanding that he doesn't *feel* he has had enough leisure time. You can help him think through things he might do to feel he is getting recreation, and then urge him to actually carry out such activities.

You will need to commit yourself to sticking by him for as long as it takes to get through this mid-life transition. How long that will be depends upon the individual situation—your husband's self-knowledge and self-esteem, his job satisfaction, his marriage satisfaction, his physical health, your understanding and help, his relationship with his children, and a whole lot of other factors. Several observers note that the total mid-life transition takes years but the actual crisis period may take from several months to a few years.[1]

CAN I HOLD ON?

My husband warns that the crisis is not like the flu.[2] A man doesn't have it for a few days and get over it. From his experience in counseling hundreds of mid-life couples over a period of twenty-two years, Jim has concluded that the unsettled period seems to average about three years, with a gradual beginning for some months, then several months or a year of acute stress, and a gradual decline for some more months. When a mid-life woman first comes to Jim for help in coping with her husband's strange behavior, he asks her to commit herself to living with the situation for as long as five years.

Don't let the length of time overwhelm you. You only have to live one day at a time! The mid-life crisis is a developmental process and it takes time, the same as adolescence takes time. When your child turns thirteen, you don't have to live the next five to seven years all at one time. You go from one day to the next until that child has one day arrived at the end of his special developmental time. He has passed from being a child to being an adult. You have good times and bad ones, but, hopefully, you both have learned a lot and grown closer to each other. Adolescence is a normal (but that doesn't mean painless!) and necessary time. So is your husband's mid-life transition.

LOVE IS SAYING YOU'RE SORRY

Once you have committed yourself to helping your husband during this time, you will want to know what to do next. There are some more helpful attitudes you need. "But I thought I worked on myself enough in the last few chapters. When do I start working on my husband?" I hear you ask.

Another important attitude you need is that of confession of sin—not your husband's, but yours. "But he's the one who has been acting like a stinker. He should ask to be forgiven, not me," you sputter.

A key to mid-life marriage restoration is your willingness to recognize that you are a part of the existing dissatisfaction. True, he is the other part. But your responsibility lies with *your* contribution to the marriage relationship. You need to confess your failures, weaknesses, stubbornnesses, insensitivities, and other faults that have undermined the happiness of your marriage. You need to tell God you are sorry and tell your husband you are sorry. Your genuine contrition for having wronged your husband is necessary for your wholeness, whether or not your husband ever sees his errors and whether or not he ever forgives you for yours. God promises you his forgiveness and lets you start over clean. "If we confess our sins, he is faithful and just to forgive us our sins, and to cleanse us from all unrighteousness" (1 John 1: 9, KJV).

HE HASN'T CONFESSED

Closely related to your asking to be forgiven is your attitude of forgiving your husband. "Wait a minute!" you protest. "I've gone out on a limb to confess my wrongs in the relationship. Now you're asking me to forgive him for his part and he hasn't even said he's sorry. Besides that, he doesn't think he's done anything wrong. Everything's my fault in his eyes."

One of the most helpful things you can do for your husband is to free him so he can change. You do this by forgiving him for all the ways in which he has offended you—even if he doesn't ask to be forgiven.

Two things happen when you forgive your husband. First, you are set free so that the problem is not eating you. When you turn over your role as judge to God, you end your responsibility to make sure your husband confesses his wrongs. Second, as you forgive your husband, he is again assured that God will forgive him. He senses that if a mere human can offer genuine forgiveness to him, certainly a loving God will forgive and restore.

HELPING GOD

It is not your place to punish your husband nor to make him feel guilty. Some of our mid-life friends keep asking us, "Do you think my husband feels guilty about what he is doing? Do you think he realizes how wrong he is?" His sensitivity to sin is God's responsibility. Your task is to forgive him and love him.

Norm Wright, associate professor of psychology at Biola College, founder of Christian Family Enrichment, and an author and family counselor, says: "Forgiveness is not forgetting. . . . is not pretending [an event never occurred]. . . . is not a feeling. . . . is not demanding a change before we forgive. . . . [and] is not easy."[3]

I latched onto his phrase, "forgiveness is not forgetting." I've always been told that true forgiveness means totally forgetting, and yet I could never completely forget some incidents in my life. Norm Wright's explanation makes sense:

> God constructed us in such a way that our brain is like a giant computer. Whatever has happened to us is stored in our memory. The remembrance will always be with us.
>
> There are, however, two different ways of remembering. One is to recall the offense or hurt in such a way that it continues to affect us and our relationship with another. It

continues to eat away and bother us so that the hurt remains. Another way of remembering simply says, "Yes, that happened. I know it did, but it no longer affects me. It's a fact of history, yet has no emotional significance or effect. It's there, but we are progressing onward at this time, and I am not hindered nor is our relationship hurt by that event." The fact remains, but it no longer entangles us in its tentacles of control.[4]

LOVE WITHOUT STRINGS

An attitude that follows forgiveness is love. You might not agree that love is an attitude if you think love is something you fall in or out of. John Powell tells us that love is not a feeling: "It would be fatal to identify love with a feeling, because of the fickleness of feelings. However, it would be equally lethal to a relationship of love if there were no warm and loving feelings to support the intentions of love."[5] Powell says that love is a "decision-commitment."

Loving your husband includes accepting him as he is at this moment. When you love your husband, you value him without strings attached. You don t say to yourself, "When he changes, I will love him," or, "If he will do thus and so, I can give myself to this relationship again." Unconditional love may not be your natural response to your husband at this time, but you can work at it. Since love is more than a feeling that simply happens without your control and since it involves your will, you can work at building love.

Love grows by cultivation, by looking at the positive qualities of the one you love, by putting yourself out to meet his needs. Contempt and hate grow by cultivation too, by looking at the negative qualities and actions of the other one, by selfishly not doing the kind things that help him. You can use your will to decide whether to love or to despise your husband.

YOUR WAY OR HIS?

When you show you love your husband, you need to do so in a way that is meaningful to him. He may not care one whit that you are using a special tablecloth, flowers, and candlelight for dinner, but you may be thinking he is really going to know you love him by your going to all the extra effort. He might prefer that you take time to watch a football game on television with him. He may not be convinced of your love for him by the special cards you give him on various occasions so much as by your withholding a scolding when he doesn't get around to washing the car.

I like the story Bruce Larson tells of the parents who learned how to show love in a meaningful way to their teenage sons who were disappointing them very much by the tough friends they had chosen to hang out with. The boys preferred skipping the church youth programs and doing things with the motorcycle crowd. There was a growing barrier between the parents and their sons.

The mother suddenly realized that she could show the tremendous love she felt for her boys by accepting and loving their friends. She invited their coarse friends to their home and made them feel welcome to come often. As a result, the relationship between the parents and sons was transformed, and eventually the leader of the gang came to know Christ. Perhaps you can think of some creative ways to express your love for your husband in a way he can understand.

You can show your husband you love him by adopting a "no nag" policy, by not manipulating him with tears, sex, or other means; and by affirming and encouraging him. The way love behaves is expressed in 1 Corinthians 13: " . . . very patient and kind, never jealous or envious, never boastful or proud, never haughty or selfish or rude . . . does not demand its own way . . . is not irritable or touchy . . . does not hold grudges and will hardly even notice when others do it wrong . . . never glad about injustice . . . loyal to him no matter what the cost . . . will always believe in him, and always stand your ground in defending him" (1 Cor. 13:4-7).

Sometimes when I start to be irritated about something Jim does that displeases me, I remember, "Love covers all transgressions" (Prov. 10:12, NASB) or, "Love forgets mistakes; . . ." (Prov. 17:9). Often there's no better way to handle an offense than to cover it with your love and forgive the offender. That doesn't mean that you cease to be assertive when assertiveness is needed. But most of us need more practice in forgiving and loving than we do in sticking up for our rights.

TUNE IN

Another helpful attitude for you to maintain during your husband's mid-life crisis is alertness. Many wives are totally unaware of the stresses their husbands are undergoing until they reach the traumatic stage. If you will be aware of the signs your husband is beginning to give at the very start of his mid-life transition, you can help minimize some of the problems. If he seems depressed, encourage him to talk. You may learn that he is beginning to feel threatened at work. He may not express that fear, however, unless you let him know you are an ally, wanting to listen to his concerns. When he does talk over his worries and feelings, be sure to empathize. Don't ridicule, criticize, or advise him. Don't give pat answers. Listen to him and encourage him.

HELPING YOUR HUSBAND

Many wives don't even know when their husbands are depressed or discouraged because they aren't paying any attention to them. You may have many valid reasons for your insensitivity—busy career, children, social obligations, just plain thoughtlessness—but the results are always negative. Your husband may not be asking for your attention, but that isn't good either. Not being aware of your hurting husband or his not looking for you to help, indicates you are drifting apart in your care and concern for each other. It is causing a separation between you that doesn't need to be there if you will only wake up and work to close the gap. Kilgore says, "To be alert, cultivate these characteristics: asking, listening, empathizing, remembering, displaying tenderness, seeing, comforting, touching, accompanying, enabling, and respecting."[6]

THE FLEXIBLE FRAU

Another state of mind that will be valuable during your husband's mid-life crisis is actually a pair of attitudes—flexibility and availability. By this time in your marriage, you have probably grown accustomed to living your own life and keeping your own schedule while your husband has been busy with his career. You may have a set pattern for how daily life is to run for each of you, and you may even think you have a pretty clear idea of how the future is going to go. Then your husband begins to act discontented and wants something different. He may start hobbies and other interests for which he never took time before. He may want you to join him in these new activities, and you'll be wise if you do. He may want to spend more time talking with you. There certainly will be some changes in his life-style, and you need to be ready to bend with them.

You should be available to him more than you ever

have been before. That may mean that you leave the kids with a baby-sitter or on their own while you go away with him for a weekend. You may find yourself attending sports equipment shows with him. You may have aching muscles you never knew you had as you take up biking with him. For me, one of the changes was sailing with Jim on his newly acquired catamaran. I'm not a natural-born sailor as he is, and relaxation for me is not dodging the boom as we tack back and forth across the undersized lakes of midstate Illinois, but I was determined to enjoy sailing!

LIFE-STYLE REVIEW

There may be other life-style changes you will make. For some women, it may be dressing to please him or changing a hairstyle. It may be developing a more carefree attitude so that you are fun to come home to. It could be making yourself more available for sexual encounters with your husband.

Some women may object to making changes and say they are denying their true selves. You need to keep your goal in perspective, however. Right now, you are wanting to help your husband successfully navigate his mid-life transition. Included in that is the improvement of your marriage and you personally. You probably will discover that most of the changes your husband would like in you are ones that also please you.

One of the life-style changes I made was to resign from teaching. I had returned to teaching part-time to help pay tuition when Barbara and Brenda chose to attend a private Christian liberal arts college. Then one year I had to accept a full-time position if I were to keep the job.

That was the year Jim went headlong into his mid-life crisis. One of his problems was lack of sufficient rest and relaxation because of the eighty to one hundred hours a week he worked as pastor of our active church. He had previously taken Mondays as his day off, but he felt guilty about relaxing a whole day while I was away working.

Because I was gone from home longer each day, my housework had to be crammed into a shorter time. I had less time for Jim if he was home in the evening. Because I needed enough rest to keep up with my students for a full day, I was very rigid about getting to sleep by a certain time each night. That often left no quiet, relaxing moments in bed to chat casually about the things that concerned each of us and to keep up with each other's world.

That spring I began to sense that my husband needed more of me than I could give him when I was teaching full-time. Still, we certainly needed the income and I was enjoying success in my profession.

God did two things for me to help me make a decision. One was a growing discontent with my work. There wasn't any good explanation. I was still successful, I still loved my students, and I enjoyed my colleagues. But I could hardly stand each half-hour of each day. I think that feeling was necessary to help me cut the ties.

God also used the Amplified version of Proverbs 31:16 to convince me that for now my place was at home so I could better provide for Jim's needs. "She considers a new field before she buys or accepts it—expanding prudently (and not courting neglect of her present duties by assuming others). With her savings (of time and strength) she plants fruitful vines in her vineyard." That told me that at this time I needed to be caring for my vineyard at home—my husband.

I still had a struggle when the time actually came to submit my resignation because of pressure from others in the profession. It was hard to believe I was simply going to stay home and work on some projects with my husband. And yet I have experienced complete peace about my decision ever since then. My expanded time at home enabled me to work with Jim doing research for, editing, and typing *Men in Mid-Life Crisis.* I am also free to participate with him at conferences and seminars. Any loss I experienced when I left my teaching position has been more than repaid by the reward and fulfillment of my new career with Jim.

BEYOND STAGNATION

One more attitude that is prudent during your husband's mid-life crisis is that of determining to grow personally—in as many ways as possible, whether spiritually, emotionally, intellectually, or in whatever way you need to expand. One reason is that you will be a better person for growing. Another is that your husband may resent anything that hints of being "old." If you are stagnant in your personal growth, you may appear to be old to him.

What are you doing to learn more about world, national, and local affairs? Today's Christian woman can't afford to be uninformed. What are the goals you have set for yourself for this next year? Perhaps you plan to study the current philosophies of womanhood and compare them to Christian principles and decide what you believe. Perhaps this is the time to enroll in that upholstering class. Have you taken Red Cross CPR lessons (cardiopulmonary resuscitation) so you might help save someone's life? Your husband, remember, is in the heart-attack period of his life!

Perhaps you have evaluated your time commitments, and right now you aren't going to take on any additional outside activities. You can still be a growing person by keeping your daily devotional time with the Lord, taking another fifteen minutes sometime during the day to read from a book that will stretch your vision in some area, and listening to a daily news broadcast. You may say you don't have time to read today's good Christian books, and so you just don't get started. But fifteen minutes a day with thirty minutes on Sunday adds up to two hours a week. It's better to read a little bit regularly and receive the input than to wait for a big block of time that may never come.

BUT HE'S MINE!

Perhaps one of the hardest attitudes for you to maintain during your husband's mid-life crisis will be relinquishment. In balance with all that you are doing to support him emotionally, to help him make wise decisions, and to improve your marriage, you also have to surrender any claim you might have on him. He still has his own will. You do not possess him.

On the one hand, you need to do all you can to help him; on the other, you need to allow him his personal independence. That doesn't mean you throw up your hands and yell at him, "Go, do whatever you want! I don't care!" It does mean that you quietly acknowledge his right to himself. Because you are "doing him a favor" by trying to help doesn't mean he owes you a favor by obeying your wishes. You can commit him to the Lord. The Holy Spirit will do a much more effective job of ministering to him in the inner man than you can by your possessiveness.

"Wow! Getting through this ordeal sure gets complicated," you say in despair. I know. I've been there. And so have lots of other women. But let's see what more we can learn about understanding and meeting that man's needs.

15
SUCCESS IN UNDERSTANDING HIS NEEDS

To understand your husband, you need to be informed about this mid-life period of his life. You can't assume that you know what his needs are if you don't know about the particular stresses of this time. Dr. Levinson, the researcher from Yale, reports from his observation of mid-life men that "this period evokes tumultuous struggles within the self and with the external world. . . . Every aspect of their lives comes into question, and they are horrified by much that is revealed. They are full of recriminations against themselves and others. They cannot go on as before, but need time to choose a new path or modify the old one."[1]

You have to allow this struggle to take place. Dr. Levinson reminds us that "he is in a normal developmental period and is working on normal mid-life tasks. The desire to question and modify his life stems from the most healthy part of the self. The doubting and searching are appropriate to this period; the real question is how best to make use of them."[2] You can be a sounding board for his questioning, if you know it's healthy for him to be doing that. If you don't, you are apt to get anxious or turn him off from sharing his search with you.

TEMPORARY TURBULENCE

You can be encouraged by knowing that this tumultuous time is temporary. Many women who have not known about the mid-life crisis have become scared when their husbands begin to behave strangely. They think they are going to be this way the rest of their lives. Some women have hurried into divorce, thinking, "He isn't the man I married, and I'm not going to stay married to him like this."

This mid-life transition is a normal, necessary stage in life, and it will pass. The mid-life upheaval lasts for a limited time. If the mid-life man does not make unwise decisions during his crisis period, life on the other side will be much calmer. Men who make rash, imprudent work changes, divorce their wives, or run away have more complications to work out after their inner emotional struggle has quieted down. If both husband and wife can see that the mid-life crisis period is temporary, they can have the courage to hang on during the rough times.

You may not know it, but one of the big spectres following most men around at this time is the feeling that they are failing at everything in their lives. If superiors or colleagues are unhappy with them at work, they feel they are somehow deficient. If they are unhappy with their type of occupation, they blame themselves for the poor choice they made in the beginning.

If you are unhappy with your husband, he feels he is failing you. If he is unhappy with you, he again feels its his fault for selecting the wrong mate. If the kids are rebellious, he senses he has failed as a father. If he is overcommitted at church or in the community, he feels he is stupid for getting so involved. If he isn't doing anything for church or community, he sees himself as a shirker. No matter what he is or isn't doing, his gloomy view of himself turns it into failure. He may not voice this feeling loudly enough so that you can discuss it openly, but if you are alert to the possibility, you can do and say those positive things that will give him more assurance of his worth and a better perspective on life.

ONE MORE LOOK

Something else you need to recognize is that during part of the crisis your husband may seem to have an urge to go back to earlier days. Sometimes the "going back" may be an attempt to make up for lacks that were present in a relationship before. If he did not get along well with a brother in his teens and twenties, he may now try to strengthen the ties. Prior to now, he may have been too busy and unconcerned about keeping in touch with his high school or college friends or relatives who lived away. Now he seems to need to reestablish old communication lines, to get a look at them again, and to learn where they are in their lives.

He may hardly have looked at the invitation for his fifteenth class reunion, but when it is time for the twenty-fifth, he will go to any length to get there. He may spend hoarded money or go several hours out of his way on a business trip to look up an old friend who is "on the

199

way." He probably will want to go back to visit the area in which he spent the most memorable time of his childhood. This is all part of the process of looking back over the territory he has covered up to this time in his life before he starts out across a new frontier.

One of the reasons it is hard to meet your husband's needs during this time is because he vacillates so much in what he wants and in what pleases him. Just when you think you have figured out what to do, he wants something different. Sometimes he wants you to mother him; at other times he will resent it. At times he wants you to be his carefree lover; other times he wants you to be a responsible housewife. Of course, we all have mood changes from time to time. But a mid-life man often has extremely wide swings in his moods. Remember that this is a very unsettled, frustrating time for him. If you can keep a certain amount of resilience in your reactions to his vacillating moods, you can cushion some of the potentially rocky times.

EVERYTHING STINKS

A major emotion your husband may display most of the time is anger. He is angry that he is getting older, angry that he feels tired, angry that his financial obligations are grinding him under, angry that he hasn't reached his career goals—or that he has and it hasn't made any difference anyway—angry that life is a big waste of time, angry that you don't understand him or do what pleases him, angry that the kids only want him for the things he can provide them, angry that no one appreciates him, angry that God has let life be this way—angry, angry, angry. When he doesn't vocalize his anger, he sits depressed with his negative emotions boiling inside.

You can help your husband know that it is all right to

feel angry. Admitting he has those feelings is one step toward healing. He doesn't need to feel guilty about having the feelings. Dr. Paul Warner reminds us that anger is not sinful but is just a feeling. All physical, emotional, and psychological feelings are normal. So is the temptation that arises from these natural feelings. "No one needs to feel guilty about the natural parts of himself. One needs to experience guilt only when one is indeed actually guilty—guilty of breaking God's moral law."[3]

If you can keep cool and objective, you can let your husband spill his angry feelings to you. That doesn't mean that you should let him physically or verbally attack you. But you can help dissipate his anger by listening to him. Make sure you can stay calm and don't inflame your husband's feelings. If you can be an objective listener, you will be vital in helping him get over his anger and get on to constructive action.

OTHER HELPS

In other sections we have talked about the importance of temporarily putting aside your own needs, accepting your husband just as he is, developing sensitivity and empathy, and communicating clearly. You can also enlist outside help. You don't have to start a huge, secretive campaign of "help me help my husband." You can, however, promote natural contact with friends who will be an encouragement and stimulation for him. You can tactfully involve your adult children and other relatives and friends in ways that will affirm him. Since *Men in Mid-Life Crisis* has been published, a few pastors have started classes or small groups for mid-life men, or couples, so they can meet to discuss their stresses and mutually strengthen each other. It would be great if every Christian Education program in every church would provide classes or retreats as another help to Christian family life.

You can encourage your husband to find suitable outlets for the urges he is feeling. Many men feel a compulsion to withdraw from everything. Help your husband find times when he really can withdraw from all responsibilities. He probably won't be able to do that for long periods or very often, but if he has a definite time set aside when he can do as he wants without meeting any obligations, this will help.

He will feel a little better for a short time and then may feel the urge to withdraw again. Help him find another opportunity to retreat. He may want to spend an evening watching television without any interruptions or even without any family member watching with him, or he may want to go for a long walk. He may want to skip attending a meeting. It is better that he drop out for short periods than hang on until he completely snaps and drops out permanently.

THE RUNAWAY

Another strong pull many men feel is to run away, escape from all their pressures. Again, it is better for a man at this time to have small, appropriate escape times than to be forced into disappearing completely and permanently in order to find relief. My husband found that it helped to get into the car and drive and drive, with no destination in mind. Sometimes he also found relief by bike riding for miles in the country. Other times he would go away for an afternoon of sailing. Once in a while we went camping in the woods for two or three days. Before this, we had never gone away except for a week or two at a time during our official vacation. Jim found it necessary during his mid-life crisis, however, to take some short breaks between the longer vacations. These would provide a temporary relief so that he could hold on again for a while.

SAILBOAT OR PORSCHE

Buying the sailboat was another way Jim allowed himself a suitable outlet for some of the feelings he was experiencing. Many mid-life men have sacrificed for their families for years and then begin to spend money lavishly on themselves. Some have never had the sports car, airplane, or boat they have wanted and now go into tremendous debt to allow themselves that luxury. They become obsessed with the need to make up for the deprivation they've felt.

I knew of Jim's growing desire to sail and to have his own boat, so I encouraged him to get one. When we spent hundreds of dollars on medical tests to learn that the cause for his passing-out spells was exhaustion, I decided the money would actually be better spent on a boat to provide the recreation he needed.

Encourage your husband to find appropriate releases from his pressures so that he doesn't have to do something extreme to provide for the needs he feels. He may not get to take long breaks or get them frequently, but help him have mini-vacations whenever he can. He may not get to own a Porsche, but perhaps your next car could be a Mustang. Simply knowing that you understand and want him to have these things will relieve some of the pressure for him.

A FRIEND INDEED

Being his best friend is one of the ways you can be a valuable asset to your husband. You will have many roles to perform—wife, housekeeper, lover, co-parent—but being his best friend is more important than all the rest.

What does a best friend do? Listens, encourages, stimulates, gives insight, is loyal, is available at all times, goes places with him, is interested in his work, shares his hobbies—and knows when to sit in silence with him.

You have the advantage of being able to prove you are a true friend because you know the most about your husband, including his weaknesses, and you are still loyal and caring. You have been with him through the years to see him grow and develop, and you can appreciate what he has put into becoming what he is now. Others may admire him when he is doing well and when he can do something for them, but you are the one person in the world who can see his worth and can stick with him when he is sour, ugly, and broken.

Your enabling force for being this best friend for your husband cannot be some great reservoir of goodness in you. It must be the power of Christ in your life. Your own strength will run out, and your own needs will cry for attention. You will have to rely on Christ. Try to imagine how Christ would love your husband, listen to him, be patient with him, and do the helpful things for him, if Christ were present in physical form. That will give you an example to follow. And we have this promise: "As the Spirit of the Lord works within us, we become more and more like him" (2 Cor. 3:18b).

As you allow God to work within you personally, your response to your husband will be more and more like that of Christ's response. You will then be in a position to help your husband work through specific, troublesome areas and become a winner.

16
HELPING HIM WIN

Dick had experienced a few ups and downs in his life. But now he had been down for so many months, he didn't feel there were any more ups left for him. When he and Rita were first married he owned and operated his own small business, which had been moderately successful. Five years ago he joined a large retail firm in the same line of business. At first he was praised for his contributions to the company and was given a promotion in the first year. Now, however, his superiors and colleagues were on his back increasingly to produce more and work longer hours. There were even hints that a younger man recently hired by the firm might be considered for his position.

Three years ago Rita had started a part-time job, working five mornings a week. She still did the housework, taught a Sunday school class, led a Bible study in her home every Thursday afternoon, was program chairman for the church woman's group, and was co-president with her husband of the married couples' fellowship of their church.

Wouldn't the fellowship be surprised if they knew how things really were between them at home! Rita had become short-tempered and impatient with everyone in the family. Dick wished she weren't so devoted to her morning job so she'd be less tense at home. But then, she had always been easily upset if things didn't go her way. He began to have trouble remembering what had ever attracted him to her. Maybe it had been a mistake to get married to her in the first place. They certainly didn't have much in common any more. She didn't seem to care that he was having trouble at work. All she was interested in was getting to her job on time, having the house clean, and being prepared for teaching her Bible study and Sunday school class.

FAILING FATHER

Three of their four children had now left home. When they were younger, Dick would have said he had a close relationship with them, but now there seemed to be a problem with every one of them. The older son, Joe, and his wife had a baby six months after they were married and Joe had dropped out of college to work. Dick still felt a wedge between Joe and him that had never been removed. There were strong indications that their daughter, Sue, was a lesbian, but she wouldn't discuss it and had grown cold toward her parents. Their second daughter, Jill, had dropped out of college to travel with a Christian musical group that seemed theologically off base. They seldom heard from her. Their youngest child, Tom, was still at home because he was supposed to be finishing high school, but he had become involved in drugs and was often on detention from school. He had already had a run-in with the law. Whenever Dick tried to talk to him, they always ended up in an argument. And this was supposed to be a Christian family!

Dick alternated between feeling sorry for himself and being angry at the whole world, God included. He had had troubles before, but now everything was awful all at one time. And he was getting tired out. His stomach hurt and his chest felt tight. He seemed to live from weekend to weekend when he could grab a little extra rest. He didn't feel like working in the yard every Saturday any more. Rita crabbed that the place was beginning to look shabby, but most of the time he just didn't care.

You can easily see why Dick would feel he was failing in every important area of his life. You can also see some things he and Rita needed to do to remedy the situation.

Now, what about your own situation? Can you step back and look at it objectively and then begin to do your part in helping bring about change where it's needed?

Mid-life men generally have battles in the areas of self-esteem, the aging process and general health, occupation, wife and family, and the place of God in their lives. They need help in all these distress areas. Correction in one helps the others to a certain extent, but they need to sense some improvement in all areas. You can be more than a not-so-innocent bystander during the "war." You can be an encourager and an enabler so that your husband is the victor in these battles.

ACCENTUATE THE POSITIVE

Because of the dust he is stirring up about other things,

your husband may not show that his self-esteem is nearly zero. He may be putting up a good front to you and others. But you can be aware that his worth is being threatened by all the forces that are bearing down on him now. When he was younger and had more stamina, he could stand the tensions, but now he is tired and everything is weighing down on him at one time. He is less able to have a balancd view of himself.

You can help him feel better about himself by giving him lots of affirmation. You must be genuine, however, because he will quickly reject phoniness. He may outwardly reject your compliments and praise, even if they are honest, but inwardly he will be storing up what you say if it is based on the truth. While he is in the doldrums, he may give you no indication that the positive things you are saying about him are doing him any good. But they are adding up inside, and when he has come through this transition time, he will openly appreciate your declarations of his value.

When every area of his life looks wobbly, you can build his confidence in himself by helping him see his strong points. Point out to him how much he has grown over the years. Let him see how his personality and talents are being used and can continue to be used in his occupation and with his family and friends. If you believe in him, he will find it easier to believe in himself.

ELIMINATE THE NEGATIVE

Compare the positive influence you can have in building up your husband's self-esteem to the destructive influence you would have if you only majored on his faults, criticized, and ridiculed. Picture two different men in your mind—one whose wife affirms him and another whose wife destroys him—and decide which one you want to have a part in forming. Don't let yourself say any negative remarks to your husband or about him. Adopt a "build-and-support only" policy.

An extra benefit from your campaign of focusing on his good points is that you will increasingly appreciate him. You will continue to find more strong qualities about him and you will have more to compliment him about. The opposite is also true. When you begin to pick at your husband's faults, you will soon see nothing but bad points. Everything about him will seem wrong. That is one reason the divorce process gets so ugly. In order to support their reasons for divorce, the husband and wife each have to point up the wrong in their mate. Soon they see nothing but bad in the other. Even when some couples would like to stop the proceedings and restore their marriage, one or both of them has majored on the other's faults so strongly that contempt is the only feeling left. Remember to practice your "build-and-support-only" policy.

AT PEACE WITH HIS BODY

You can't keep your husband's body from getting older, but you can help him feel good about his physical appearance. Instead of making remarks about the paunch around his waist or his graying hair, you can tell him how attractive he is to you. Remember that many younger women are fascinated by older men. Look at your husband through the eyes of a twenty-five-year-old and see what characteristics she would admire about him. Then be sure to tell him specifically the ways in which he looks good to you.

You should encourage your husband to have a good

medical examination. He may not have done so for years, if ever. At this time, men begin to worry about symptoms they feel which they previously have ignored. With their consciousness of aging, some men become almost obsessed with the possibility of impending death. They fear heart attacks and other serious ailments because they know they now have entered the time of life when such illnesses are more likely to occur.

A thorough physical examination will put your husband's mind at rest or tell him what needs to be remedied. Some problems that could become serious might be prevented or lessened if detected and treated early.

You can, of course, help your husband's health by providing nutritious meals and especially by keeping down his calorie intake. I know it's fun to cook and bake all those yummy dishes. But you don't do your husband a favor by overfeeding him. In fact, you increase his risk of heart attack and other problems. He probably needs vitamin and mineral supplements during this time of extra stress. For example, there is strong evidence that a lack in the B vitamins contributes to fatigue, depression, irritability, anxiety, confusion, and restlessness.[1]

"Wow!" I hear you exclaim, "I'm going to get some vitamin B right now and get my husband straightened out!"

But before you get too excited, remember that the B vitamins are not a cure-all. They are worth trying, however, as an aid to better health. Our physician recommended that Jim take Stresstabs, a high potency vitamin B capsule.

You should also encourage your husband to start an exercise program. Perhaps you can find something the two of you like to do together. That could be part of the extra time you spend with each other.

Also help him get sufficient rest. The pressure he is

undergoing will be somewhat easier to take and problems won't seem so big if he is not physically tired. Rest comes not only from the hours he spends in bed but also in leisure activities when he can set aside his cares for a while. You can help by not planning jobs for him to do or by not discussing heavy matters with him every time he gets a chance to sit down.

Your husband may be overly sensitive about his aging and his changing physical appearance for a few years. He may agree with Paul's statement, "How weary we grow of our present bodies"! He can also take hope with Paul, that, "when we die and leave these bodies—we will have wonderful new bodies in heaven." And, "though our bodies are dying, our inner strength in the Lord is growing every day" (2 Cor. 5: 2a, 1b; 4: 16).

WORK WEIGHTS

Another important area of your husband's life in which he is probably fighting some battles is his occupation. Some men are dissatisfied with the type of work they are doing. Others fear losing their jobs. Still others are simply tired of having to work so hard. You need to be alert to whatever your husband expresses about his work and encourage him to talk more about it.

If he is dissatisfied with his job, help him think through alternatives. Let him know that you support him if he decides to change jobs. Sometimes men don't actually end up making major job changes, but knowing you are on his side if he would do so will relieve part of the pressure he is under.

The fear of losing his job may be real or imagined. When he is depressed, he may inaccurately sense that his job is being threatened. You can perhaps give him a better perception of the true situation.

If your husband needs to cut down on the amount of work he is doing or needs to make a change, encourage him to do some thoughtful evaluating. His self-esteem will suffer more if he makes hasty, unwise decisions that he will later regret. Help him consider the advantages and disadvantages of a job change. Let him bounce ideas off you. Perhaps he could use the help from books such as *What Color Is Your Parachute?* 2 and *Where Do I Go From Here with My Life?*[3] which give good insights into how to change careers wisely.

Whatever your husband's occupation, you should be interested in what he is doing. It may be in a field where you have absolutely no talent and little knowledge, but you can encourage him to share as much as is appropriate with you. He can at least tell you his feelings and how the job affects him.

Some husbands' work is the kind in which their wives can be involved. If that is appropriate in your case, do what you can to make yourself available to help your husband.

Whether or not his occupation is one in which you can be involved, be his ally and best friend as he works through whatever struggles he may be having with it. Let him know you are right there beside him if he decides it is best to change or cut down.

We know some families who have moved into smaller housing so that the husband could afford to cut back on his work hours. In other family situations the wives have gone to work outside the home to help with income when their husbands changed to lower-paying jobs.

WILL HE STAY?

Your husband also has some adjusting to do in regard to the family. As we have said, this era has a high divorce

212

rate. Many of the divorces could be avoided if both the husband and the wife knew how to work together on the particular problems of this age. Much of this book has been aimed at helping your marriage.

You need to be reminded that your mid-life husband must evaluate *every* part of his life. Deciding whether or not he is going to stay married to you is a necessary task. Some men quickly decide that they want the marriage to continue, with perhaps some improvements. For others, however, the decision is more of a struggle.

Ultimately, your husband will have to answer this question himself. Your part is to pray for God to work within him, to do what you can to change personally, and to encourage him by understanding and meeting his needs.

I would like to be able to say optimistically that everyone of you can be a winner with your husband in this struggle. Realistically, though, I know that some of you are on the verge of losing and others of you have already lost.

The problem is that there are two of you involved in the decision, and you can't make your husband do what he will not do. My heart aches for those of you who have a breaking or broken marriage. I wish it were in my power to give you a whole and happy relationship with your husband. Your job now, however, is to build as complete and healthy a life as possible. Much of chapters 7 through 13 are still important for you even if you become single again.

THE STALL

For those of you whose husbands have not actually divorced you, I want to encourage you not to give up hope. Many men verbally threaten divorce and do not actually start the necessary legal proceedings. Others go so far as to start but delay along the way. We have found that often these men really do not want a divorce. If you don't push them into hurrying up the procedure, a restoration may take place. Some husbands are in utter confusion. They don't know what they want.

Another woman may be pushing your husband into divorcing you so that he will be free for her. But he may also be having second thoughts about whether he wants to get married to her or anyone else. If you want to preserve your marriage, do what you can to stall a divorce action. And in the meantime do the good, positive things you can to win back your husband.

THE GIRL FRIEND ROLE

If your husband has left you, or if he is having an affair, you should relate to him as if you were in the dating stage of your relationship once again. You should behave as if you were his girl friend. That means you don't make any demands on him, you are on your best behavior around him, you dress to attract him, you do whatever it was that drew him to you during your courtship days.

He doesn't want a hovering mother or a nagging wife. He yearns for the exhilaration of a girl friend. If you provide that, he is less likely to seek it elsewhere. That is also a good attitude for you to take even if your marriage is not so threatened.

You might like to know the results of one study on traits men do and don't like in women:

Men DO like:
—A sense of humor. This adds fun to everyday life, no matter how hectic it is.
—Kindness, gentleness.
—They like makeup if they don't know you have it on—or

at least if it is natural enough to look real, and they even enjoy a bit of dramatization on special occasions.

—A good figure, but curves, not thinness.

—They are drawn to vitality and aliveness, but not to the woman who is the "life of the party."

—They appreciate tact in a woman—her talent to smooth hectic situations.

—Most of all they like a woman who makes life seem easy and uncomplicated.

—Naturalness.

Men DON'T like:

—Cattiness, snide remarks about another woman.

—They do not like new styles at first, but usually like them after they become accustomed to them.

—They hate complaining, but enjoy household chatter if it is humorous or interesting.

—They do not like the siren type. She makes them feel uneasy.

—They do not like to hear about your former conquests.

—They have a horror of becoming involved in long, emotional discussions.

—Generally, they do not like candlelight at the dinner table but succumb to it with enthusiasm if the mood of festivity or relaxation and good conversation go along with it. Otherwise, they want to see their food clearly so they can concentrate on it.

—Fretting drives them crazy.[4]

CHANGING OF THE GUARD

At this time there are other aspects of family life to which your husband must adapt. Gould points out that a role change takes place with a mid-life couple's parents and with their children. By this age it is clear that our parents are no longer our protectors and that "we are the only, the final authority over the conduct of our own lives. . . .

215

the world now belongs to us and our generation."[5] We have to control our own lives; our parents cannot do it for us. They cannot watch out for us, and we don't want them to. Yet there is a feeling of loss when we realize no one is going to care for us.

Gould continues,

> As our family changes over our mid-life years, power shifts accelerate. Our parents hang on to whatever power they have over us to fortify their sense of safety; we hang on to power over our children for the same reason. . . . It's not malice that moves us to hold on to power over our late-teenage children, and it's often not love; it's an attempt to keep our own feeling of safety intact.[6]

We don't like to feel we aren't needed by our children as much anymore.

A mid-life man may be unaware that these changes are taking place until they are very advanced; then he is stunned by the differences in the way life is now compared to when he last looked. If you and your husband can be talking about these changes in your children and your parents as they happen gradually, the adjustment will be less dramatic.

SPIRITUAL DECISIONS

At mid-life a man generally does some evaluating about his spiritual life, also. Some solid Christian men wrestle with doubts and questions that never occurred to them before or that they thought they had settled earlier. They wonder about God's genuine care for them, his sovereignty, and the value of keeping moral standards. Some may grow cold and careless in their contact with God and increasingly withdraw from fellowship with him.

Other men, who have never been believers, find God

for the first time. Some men go back to their childhood religious experience, hoping to find solace and direction there. One man we know decided once again to follow his Jewish faith after he had ignored it for many years. He became so religious his wife divorced him!

If you are a committed Christian, you are no doubt eager for your husband to experience a true, vital relationship with Jesus Christ, whether he is already a Christian or not. You know that his life—and yours—will be at its best when he is walking in the power and joy of the Lord. That is a commendable desire, but be careful! Many a zealous wife has mistakenly felt she was doing God's will by forcing her husband to a spiritual decision. It *is* God's will for your husband to be a Christian and to live as one. But it *is not* God's will for you to force that commitment on your husband.

Even the best Christian husband will have trouble swallowing a superpious attitude from you while he is struggling with the swirling issues of his mid-life crisis. Remember, he feels that he is failing in everything, and if you are throwing around all your spirituality, he is going to be sickened by it. You may be receiving neat insights from the Bible, but be careful how you share them with your husband. Keep learning from the Lord, but also ask God to control when, how, and if you should talk about it with your husband. We are reminded in 1 Peter 3:1 that our husbands will more likely be influenced by our "godly life" than by our words.

GOD CAN BE TRUSTED

Your husband will need to make his own decision about how he is going to relate to God. You can whet his appetite by the kind of life you live, but you can't force him to partake. Let God be the one to do the convincing.

217

God's Spirit working quietly inside him will do more good than all the noise you make from the outside. You can claim the principle of Philippians 2:13 to work for your husband's spiritual life: "For it is God [not your wife] who works in you to will and to act according to his good purpose" (NIV).

If your husband is a Christian who is wavering, you can take hope in the assurance of Philippians 1:6, "Being confident of this, that he who began a good work in you will carry it on to completion until the day of Christ Jesus" (NIV). You can pray with faith for your husband when he perhaps is too weak to pray for himself.

There were times when Jim didn't have any emotional energy left to pray for the help he needed. He was like a car with a dead battery, four flat tires, and no gas. When I sensed those times, I could be the one who interceded for him and claimed the promises he would have appropriated if he'd had the strength.

Spiritual decisions have to be made in the inner person. Your husband will arrive at his own level of faith and commitment to God as a result of his personal response to God's work within him. Although you cannot force the outcome of his decision, you can be an influence by your prayers and your winsome life. God promises that your supportive presence will be a help to him: "Two can accomplish more than twice as much as one, for the results can be much better. If one falls, the other pulls him up; but if a man falls when he is alone, he's in trouble" (Eccl. 4:9-10).

If your husband has been gone and now it looks as if he may come home, you may have many questions about how to relate to him. Let me share a conversation with one woman who faced such a situation.

17
AIDING HIS REENTRY

Billie had asked me to help her.

She began, "I've talked to you a lot about my fear that my husband would never come back. Well, over the past few months he and I have been talking more and the last three weeks he's been at the house for several meals. Now I'm afraid, because I'm not sure what to do. He seems to be coming back. How do I handle it all? What are the neighbors going to think?"

She paused, then added, "I have a whole new batch of questions and problems that I didn't have before. I thought it would be easy. Vince would decide to give up his girl friend and come home and that would be that. But now I see that it's perhaps even more complicated than his leaving. What do I do?"

REALITY

A husband's reentry into the home *can* be almost as difficult as his leaving. Many new adaptations are needed. Neither husband nor wife are dealing with the same old circumstances or the same people. Each person has grown and changed. It's a whole new mix, and a wife must be careful not to make assumptions that simply because her husband comes through the front door with his suitcase, everything is automatically going to be like the good old days.

In fact, if everything does go back to the good old days, the two of them will be in trouble again. It was partly the circumstances of previous days that caused her husband to leave, so hopefully the change in everyone will result in a more satisfying marriage and homelife for each person.

Some cautions at this point are necessary. A wife shouldn't be overly anxious to have her husband back. Be sure the decision is his. She should make sure that he is not being pressured or coerced so that he is returning against his will. On the other hand, she should also make sure she doesn't become his doormat. It would be better if he stayed away a little longer and thoroughly worked through his problems, perhaps with a counselor, so that when he comes back he is ready to work and to give as well as take.

EATING HUMBLE PIE

One of the big reentry problems for the husband is loss of face. When he left, he burned a good many of his bridges, thinking he might never be back and he might never have to relate to certain people again. He may have cut himself off from neighbors, people at church, and other friends when he started his new life-style. As he tries to make his way back now, he may feel humiliated. He may feel that he has to constantly give explanations to people.

At this point a wife can be very helpful. Or she can stick the knife to him. If she feels that he ought to make public apologies or come crawling back on his hands and knees, begging her forgiveness, then she is likely to exploit the situation and enjoy her position over him. He may feel too battered to go through the humiliation and she will probably lose him again.

She can, however, make it easy for her husband to return. When he visits one night for dinner, she could make it convenient for him to stay over. They could go for a walk together and express affection (not clutchiness with a sense of "Aha! I have him now!" but, "It's just good to be together!"). Then she could suggest, "Since it's late, maybe you'd like to just sleep here. If you'd feel more comfortable, you can use the guest room. We'll set the alarm, and you can be up and showered before the kids are awake, so they don't get any wrong ideas that you're moving back permanently. I also want you to know that if you sleep over tonight that doesn't mean I think you're going to move back. It's just that I like to be with you."

If her husband does decide to move back, the two of them must talk together about how to handle his return with neighbors, friends, and church people. Maybe they'll decide to have a party at their house and announce that they are back together again. Most couples, however, let the word get around quietly, spearheaded mostly by the wife who shares the simple information in a positive way, "It's good to have my husband back again, and he's so glad to be back." There may be some sticky relationships, but as the couple talks together about how to handle them and invites God to be involved in the process, they will find that most people are delighted that their marriage has been reunited.

NO FENCE-SITTING

Another problem created by reentry is the husband's need to cut off his old relationships in the single world as he moves back into the married world. Once again he has the problem of losing face. He may have told people that he was in the process of getting a divorce, and he may have dated several women or may have been involved in an affair with another woman.

This detour has to be brought to a conclusion. The reentry will not be successful if the husband tries to keep one foot in each of the two worlds. That's why it's important for him to be sure that he really wants to be back. He must make a clean break with his temporary bachelorhood. A wife can be supportive, but she has to be careful not to be naggy. He is the one to tell the singles that he is back in a relationship with his family. She can help best by praying and encouraging him so that he feels strong enough to make the break.

In *Men in Mid-Life Crisis* Jim talks about getting out of the affair and says that affairs break up because they are not meeting a person's needs. When a husband's affair reaches the point where it is no longer satisfying, he will probably again evaluate what he really wants in life and begin to prioritize his needs and values. When he decides to return home, it will help his adjustment if he makes a clean break with his short-lived single life.

PRACTICALITIES

After I had talked generally with Billie about her husband's reentry, she was still loaded with questions.

"Will I ever be able to trust him again?" she asked.

"Billie, remember how trust grew the first time. When you first met, you didn't have a full-grown relationship of trust. Your trust grew as you spent more time with each other and learned about each other. Trust will return again by the same process. Remember, also, that you and your husband are not alone. God is involved and is going to be ministering to each one of you."

"What do I do if, after he's moved everything back into the house, I find an old note or a ticket stub from a date he had while he was gone? Do I confront him with it?"

"No, just let it go. It's part of the past. You've forgiven him. You've decided to make a new go of your marriage. Let that old thing die. Commit it to God's care. You may be tempted to distrust Vince and seeing that old note or ticket stub may bring you to the point of anger, but you can let go of it because of the grace of God."

"What if *she* calls again or writes a letter?" Billie grimaced.

"Assure Vince that you love him, but let him handle her. It's his responsibility to make the break with his past. Go to God for strength and ask him to meet the needs of the other woman so she doesn't feel driven to try to take Vince away."

"What if he gets restless and wants to go again?"

"Remember that the reentry transition is likely to take from a couple of months to a year or more. Also remember that when you first met Vince, you were not ready to get married, and when you were first married, you needed time to adjust to living together. An adjustment period is necessary now. During this time he may feel restless. Assure him that if he needs to go for a ride, he should feel free to do that. If he needs to be alone in the house, provide that opportunity. Or if he wants to go someplace with just you, make arrangements to go. And continually trust him to God during this reentry transition."

Then Billie said, "I've changed a lot since he left. I'm a

more independent woman. Do I revert to becoming dependent again?"

"No, one of the things that is attracting Vince to you is that you've done some growing and that you are more independent. He likes you better that way. Remember also that he's changed. You will have to spend some time talking to each other to find out how you've each changed so that you can learn to adapt to the new people you are."

"Sometimes," I continued, "a wife has been so cautious in dealing with her husband during the early stages of his mid-life crisis that she has never told him any of her personal feelings. If the marriage is to work again, however, you and your husband must both share your feelings. That doesn't mean that the first night he comes back you dump everything on him, but it does mean that you move increasingly toward sharing who you are and how you've changed. You need to share what you feel and what's going on inside of you. This permission to share doesn't mean that you bring up the past. It does mean that you share who you are now and what God has been doing to you."

MORE VITAL ISSUES

Billie then brought up the subject of their children. "I can see that the kids are happy about the prospects of Vince's return, but I also can sense that they are afraid it might be only temporary."

"You can dispel their fears by telling them that God loves each one of the family, that dad has been struggling with some problems but is working through those things. Calm them by saying that it looks as if you are going to be a family again. You also can assure them that dad loves each one of them and that you do, too. Tell them that God is going to continue to care for your entire family."

Then Billie said, "Sometimes I wake up in the middle of the night crying, because I realize that he is having sex with another person. Now I ask myself what it will be like the first time that he wants to have sex with me again. Will that nightmare cause me to be frigid? How can I ever give myself to him again?"

"When you first met, you didn't jump into bed together. You probably had months and months of getting to know each other. You expressed care and tenderness for each other, and then, after you were married, it was an easy step—a strongly desired step—to have sexual intercourse. Follow that same pattern now. Tell him frankly of your fears, and also tell him that you don't want that to put him off, but you need time.

Counselors who work with couples experiencing sexual problems recommend that a couple should first of all agree that they will not have sexual intercourse until both of them equally desire it. Until then, the relationship will be one of hugging, kissing, assuring each other, building each other's emotional strength, petting, and touching, but there is to be no sense of obligation. This freedom from obligation allows the emotions to be free. In the setting of growing trust and greater expression of love and caring, the old sexual desires will fully return."

"Can I forgive him after all I've been through?"

"Yes, you can, because God has forgiven you after all he's been through for you. You can forgive Vince because your children need you to forgive him. You must forgive him because, unless you do, he will be gone again. And this time it won't be his problem, but yours. If you hold onto an unforgiving spirit to protect yourself from hurt, you will be hurt again.

"If you hold onto an unforgiving spirit in order to have a club to strike back at him later on, that club will beat your marriage to death. You will use it for every unrelated minor sin that your husband commits for the rest of his life. Billie, you must decide to ask God to forgive you for any part that you had in your marital problem and ask God to give you the grace to forgive Vince. Then forgive him totally, and give up completely any opportunity to ever bring it up again."

You can see from this conversation that there will be many adjustments if your husband comes home again, but this homecoming is probably what you have wanted more than anything else! The realignment period may not be easy, but the promise of good years ahead together and God's strength will help the effort.

18

MORE THAN CONQUERORS

For most men—and their wives—the mid-life crisis can be the most difficult experience they have had so far in life. More changes are taking place in a shorter period of time than ever before, and at the same time the man is confronted with aging and the need for a reevaluation of every area of his life. He is undergoing giant changes in his life, many of them losses of one kind or another, and at a time when he is less emotionally and physically able to handle the stress.

Many young adults ask what they can do to prevent the mid-life crisis. As you talk with younger couples, you can tell them that this time in life cannot be avoided any more than adolescence can. But they can be preparing themselves so the crisis is less severe and so they will be more apt to come through it successfully.

The young adult should select an occupation that matches his abilities and interests. A young man may get pushed into a profession that pleases his parents or some other influential person in his life but is not in line with the kind of person he is or the gifts God has given to him. Sometimes a man gets locked into a job because it provides the income he needs at the moment, but it may not be what he really wants to do for the rest of his life. He may put up with it for years. But at mid-life an ill-suited job will greatly increase his stress.

Having gone through the mid-life trauma yourself, you can point out to younger couples that they need to be building a strong marriage during all the years before mid-life. Problem areas should be worked out as they arise, not ignored until they become monumental about the time everything else is happening at mid-life. A couple should be learning to communicate frequently and adequately with each other and should earnestly be trying to meet each other's needs.

Other areas to be worked on before mid-life include proper exercise, a pattern of regular relaxation, and an honest self-knowledge accompanied with a high self-esteem. Of course, a strong, vital relationship with God is very important. The more of God's Word a man has practiced appropriating for his daily life and the more he has experienced God's care and faithfulness all through life, the greater store of resources he will have when his mid-life difficulties hit.

HOPE FOR THE FUTURE

The exciting thing both you and your husband need to know is that once the mid-life transition has been successfully made, there is a better life ahead. I am not saying this simply to encourage you through a rough time or because Christians are supposed to be optimistic. Many experts in sociology and psychology agree that once a man has settled most of the pressing issues—his aging, his occupation, his marriage—he enters a long, peaceful period.[1]

The post mid-life man is more optimistic about life in general. He sees that his wisdom and experience are as valuable as physical strength and stamina were in his youth. He is generally more congenial at work. Instead of feeling competitive with younger men, he now becomes generative. That is, he enjoys passing on to others what he knows and he does what he can to help others succeed. He chooses and keeps friends on the basis of mutual love and appreciation rather than what they can do for him. He becomes a more gentle, mellow man. As a husband, he is more tender and thoughtful. He is also a better lover and takes time to be sentimental and romantic.

Jim and I know from our own experience that these good changes really do happen! They happened for us, and we know other couples who have also experienced these good results after the mid-life crisis. Marriages can become stronger and more satisfying if both of you have "hung in there" during the rough times and have not made the irreparable decision to give up. Many marriages have been restored even after couples have been separated for a time. Couples once again enjoy the delight of a truly happy, satisfying relationship with each other.

"In all these things we are more than conquerors through him who loved us" (Rom. 8:37, NIV).

The word "conqueror" suggests that there was a battle. The battle wasn't *eliminated* through him who loved us. It had to be fought, but it was *won!*

NOTES

CHAPTER ONE

1. Jim Conway, *Men in Mid-Life Crisis* (Elgin, Ill.: David C. Cook Publishing Co., 1978), pp. 11-12, 299-301.

CHAPTER TWO

1. Daniel J. Levinson, et al., *The Seasons of a Man's Life* (New York: Alfred A. Knopf, 1978; New York: Ballantine Books, 1979).
2. Bernice L. Neugarten, ed., *Personality in Middle and Late Life* (New York: Atherton Press, 1964).
3. Alan B. Knox, *Adult Development and Learning* (San Francisco: Jossey-Bass Publishers, 1977).
4. Roger L. Gould, *Transformations–Growth and Change in Adult Life* (New York: Simon & Schuster, 1978).
5. Jim Conway, *Men in Mid-Life Crisis.*
6. Ibid., p. 17.
7. Ibid., pp. 17-18.
8. Howard J. Clinebell, Jr., *Growth Counseling for Mid-Years Couples* (Philadelphia: Fortress Press, 1977), pp. 2-3.
9. Levinson, p. 199.
10. Edmund Bergler, *The Revolt of the Middle-Aged Man* (New York: A. A. Wyn, 1954), pp. 117-118.
11. Alvin R. Voelkner, "Challenge for Church: A Middle-Aged Majority," *Our Sunday Visitor,* Feb. 23, 1975, p. 10.
12. Levinson, pp. 23, 191.
13. Gould, p. 217.
14. James E. Kilgore, *Try Marriage Before Divorce* (Waco, Tex.: Word Books, 1978), p. 73.

CHAPTER THREE

1. Daniel J. Levinson, et al., *The Seasons of a Man's Life,* p. 199.
2. "The Mid-Life Crisis," *Ebony,* April 1979, p. 82.
3. Levinson, p. 28.
4. Ibid., p. 199. Italics are the author's.
5. Kenneth D. Feigenbaum, Antioch College, Columbia, Maryland, "Mid-Life Crisis of Males," Lecture delivered at the University of Illinois, Bevier Hall, February 15, 1979.

CHAPTER FOUR

1. William J. Lederer and Don D. Jackson, *The Mirages of Marriage* (New

YOU AND YOUR HUSBAND'S MID-LIFE CRISIS

York: W. W. Norton, 1968), pp. 87-90.

2. Jim Conway, *Men in Mid-Life Crisis,* pp. 159, 283-287.

3. Ibid., pp. 157-165; Gail Sheehy, *Passages* (New York: Dutton, 1976), pp. 376-393.

4. Sheehy, p. 377.

5. Tim LaHaye, *Understanding the Male Temperament* (Old Tappan, N. J.: Fleming H. Revell, 1977), p. 176.

CHAPTER FIVE

1. Gail Sheehy, *Passages,* pp. 440-464.

CHAPTER SIX

1. Roger L. Gould, "Phases of Adult Life," *American Journal of Psychiatry* 129: 5 (Nov. 1972), p. 528.

2. Don Williams, *The Apostle Paul & Women in the Church* (Glendale, Cal.: Regal, 1977); Dorothy R. Pape, *In Search of God's Ideal Woman* (Downers Grove, Ill.: InterVarsity Press, 1976); Richard and Joyce Boldrey, *Chauvinist or Feminist? Paul's View of Women* (Grand Rapids: Baker Book House, 1976); Letha Scanzoni and Nancy Hardesty, *All We're Meant to Be* (Waco, Tex.: Word Books, 1974); Herbert and Fern Harrington Miles, *Husband-Wife Equality* (Old Tappan, N. J.: Fleming H. Revell, 1978).

CHAPTER SEVEN

1. James E. Kilgore, *Try Marriage Before Divorce,* pp. 17-18.

2. Kilgore, pp. 146-148; Conway, *Men in Mid-Life Crisis,* pp. 220-240.

3. Kilgore, p. 148.

4. Natalie Gittelson, "Infidelity—Can You Forgive and Forget?" *Redbook,* November 1978, p. 189.

5. Archibald D. Hart, *Feeling Free* (Old Tappan, N. J.: Fleming H. Revell, 1979).

6. Paul L. Warner, *Feeling Good About Feeling Bad* (Waco, Tex.: Word Books, 1979).

7. Andre Bustanoby, *But I Didn't Want a Divorce* (Grand Rapids: Zondervan, 1978), pp. 80-81.

8. Gittelson, p. 191.

9. Gittelson, p. 191.

10. Kilgore, p. 73.

11. Kilgore.

12. Matt. 9: 20-22; Mark 5: 25-34.

CHAPTER EIGHT

1. *Vital Statistics of the U.S.,* U.S. Dept. of Health, Education, & Welfare, Health Statistics, 1975.

2. Psalm 62: 8.

3. Robert F. Winch, *Mate Selection: A Study of Complementary Needs* (New York: *Harper,* 1958).

CHAPTER NINE

1. H. S. Vigeveno and Anne Claire,*Divorce and the Children* (Glendale, Cal.: Regal, 1979), p. 44.
2. Ibid., p. 47.
3. Judith S. Wallerstein and Joan B. Kelly, *Surviving the Break-Up: How Children Actually Cope with Divorce,* as quoted by Marilyn Murray Willison, "Children of Divorce," *Family Weekly,* March 2, 1980, p. 6.
4. Andre Bustanoby, *But I Didn't Want a Divorce* (Grand Rapids: Zondervan, 1978).
5. Vigeveno and Claire.
6. Ibid., pp. 49-52.

CHAPTER TEN

1. John 14:27 (NASB).
2. John 16:33 (NASB).
3. Titus 2:14; Rom. 3:23-24.
4. Eph. 1:5-7.
5. Rom. 8:16-17; Gal. 4:7.
6. John 3:3-7.
7. John 1:4, 8:12, 10:10, 14:6; 2 Cor. 5:17.
8. John 3:36, 6:40,47, 1 John 5:12.
9. 1 John 1:9.
10. Heb. 4:16.
11. John Powell, *The Secret of Staying in Love* (Niles, Ill.: Argus, 1974), pp. 64-66.

CHAPTER ELEVEN

1. James Dobson, *What Wives Wish Their Husbands Knew About Women* (Wheaton, Ill.: Tyndale House, 1975), p. 147.
2. Ibid., pp. 143-156.
3. Joyce Brothers,*Better Than Ever* (New York: Simon & Schuster, 1975), p. 169.
4. Ibid., p. 162.
5. Ibid., p. 169.
6. Dobson, pp. 151-153.
7. Archibald D. Hart,*Feeling Free* (Old Tappan, N.J.: Revell, 1979), p. 119.
8. Gladys Hunt,*Ms. Means Myself* (Grand Rapids: Zondervan, 1972), p. 17.
9. Hart, pp. 125-126.
10. Ibid., pp. 126-128.
11. Ibid., pp. 128-131.
12. Ibid., pp. 80-88.
13. U.S. Dept. of Vital Statistics and U.S. Dept. of Labor, as quoted by

YOU AND YOUR HUSBAND'S MID-LIFE CRISIS

Connie Rae, "Women Are Different," *Today's Christian Woman*, Fall/Winter 1978-79, p. 85.

14. Dennis and Ruth Gibson, "Speaking Up to Your Husband," *Today's Christian Woman*, Fall/Winter 1978-79, p. 36.

15. David Augsburger, *Caring Enough to Confront* (Glendale, Cal.: Regal, 1973), p. 3.

16. Kilgore, *Try Marriage Before Divorce*, p. 80.

17. Ibid., p. 79.

18. John E. Gibson, "Can Humor Affect Friendship?" *Family Weekly*, February 24, 1980, p. 17.

19. Ibid.

20. Ibid.

CHAPTER TWELVE

1. Peter E. Gillquist, *Love Is Now* (Grand Rapids: Zondervan, 1970).

2. Robert L. Wise, *When There Is No Miracle* (Glendale, Cal.: Regal, 1977).

3. Philip Yancey, *Where Is God When It Hurts?* (Grand Rapids: Zondervan, 1977).

4. John Powell, *The Secret of Staying in Love*, p. 48.

5. Alan Loy McGinnis, *The Friendship Factor* (Minneapolis: Augsburg, 1979), esp. Ch. 6.

6. Lillian E. Troll, Joan Israel, and Kenneth Israel, eds., *Looking Ahead* (Englewood Cliffs, N. J.: Prentice-Hall, 1977), pp. 106-108. (Italics mine.)

7. Bruce Larson, *No Longer Strangers* (Waco, Tex.: Word Books, 1971), pp. 105-106.

CHAPTER THIRTEEN

1. Sally Conway, "Meditations of a Mid-life Wife," unpublished poem, 1980.

2. Joyce Landorf, *The Fragrance of Beauty* (Wheaton, Ill.: Victor Books, 1973), pp. 13-24.

3. Troll, Israel, and Israel, *Looking Ahead*, pp. 59-64.

4. Troll, Israel, and Israel, p. 90.

5. Troll, Israel, and Israel, p. 21.

6. Landorf, p. 20.

7. Gloria Heidi, *Winning the Age Game* (Garden City, N. Y.: Doubleday & Co.; A & W Visual Library, 1976).

8. Anne Ortlund, *Disciplines of the Beautiful Woman* (Waco, Tex.: Word Books, 1977).

9. Heidi, pp. 151-152.

10. Josephine Lowman, "Why Grow Old?", *The Champaign-Urbana, Ill., News-Gazette*, January 24, 1980.

11. Herbert and Fern Miles, *Husband-Wife Equality* (Old Tappan, N. J.: Revell, 1978).

12. Don Williams, *The Apostle Paul and Women in the Church* (Glendale, Cal.: Regal, 1979).

13. Dorothy Pape, *In Search of God's Ideal Woman: A Personal Examination of the New Testament* (Downers Grove, Ill.: InterVarsity Press, 1976).

14. Richard and Joyce Boldrey, *Chauvinist or Feminist? Paul's View of Women* (Grand Rapids, Mich.: Baker, 1976).
15. Letha Scanzoni and Nancy Hardesty, *All We're Meant to Be: A Biblical Approach to Women's Liberation* (Waco, Tex.: Word, 1975).
16. Hunt, *Ms. Means Myself*, p. 25.
17. Troll, Israel, and Israel, p. 31.
18. Ingrid Trobisch, *The Joy of Being a Woman* (New York: Harper & Row, 1975), p. 2.

CHAPTER FOURTEEN

1. Daniel J. Levinson, et al., *The Seasons of a Man's Life*, p. 191; Gould, *Transformations*, pp. 217-307; Jim Conway, *Men in Mid-Life Crisis*, pp. 144-154.
2. Conway, pp. 283-285.
3. H. Norman Wright, "I'll Never Forgive You!" *Family Life Today* (Glendale, Cal.: Gospel Light), VI: 2, January 1980, pp. 16-17.
4. Ibid., p. 16.
5. John Powell, *The Secret of Staying in Love*, p. 47.
6. James Kilgore, *Try Marriage Before Divorce*, p. 79.

CHAPTER FIFTEEN

1. Daniel J. Levinson, et al., *The Seasons of a Man's Life*, p. 199.
2. Ibid.
3. Paul L. Warner, *Feeling Good About Feeling Bad*, pp. 45, 15-16.

CHAPTER SIXTEEN

1. Gloria Heidi, *Winning the Age Game*, p. 245.
2. Richard Nelson Bolles, *What Color Is Your Parachute?* (San Francisco: Ten Speed, 1970; 2nd ed., 1977).
3. John C. Crystal and Richard N. Bolles, *Where Do I Go from Here with My Life?* (New York: Seabury, 1974).
4. Josephine Lowman, "Why Grow Old?" *The Champaign-Urbana, Ill., News-Gazette*, January 24, 1980.
5. Roger L. Gould, *Transformations*, pp. 220-225.

CHAPTER EIGHTEEN

1. Conway, pp. 152-153; Gould, *Transformations;* Levinson, et al., *The Seasons of a Man's Life;* Joel and Lois Davitz, *Making It from Forty to Fifty* (New York: Random House, 1976); Eda J. LeShan, *The Wonderful Crisis of Middle Age* (New York: David McKay, 1973).

SUGGESTED
READING LIST

WOMANHOOD

Richard and Joyce Boldrey, *Chauvinist or Feminist? Paul's View of Women* (Grand Rapids, Baker Book House, 1976).

Gloria Heidi, *Winning the Age Game* (Garden City, N.Y.: Doubleday, A and W Visual Library, 1976).

Jeanne Hendricks, *A Woman for All Seasons* (Nashville: Thomas Nelson, Inc., 1977).

Gladys Hunt, *Ms. Means Myself* (Grand Rapids: Zondervan, 1972).

Joyce Landorf, *The Fragrance of Beauty* (Wheaton, Ill.: Victor Books, 1973).

Anne Ortlund, *Disciplines of the Beautiful Woman* (Waco, Tex.: Word Books, 1977).

Dorothy R. Pape, *In Search of God's Ideal Woman* (Downers Grove, Ill.: InterVarsity Press, 1976).

Letha Scanzoni and Nancy Hardesty, *All We're Meant to Be* (Waco, Tex.: Word Books, 1974).

Ingrid Trobisch, *The Joy of Being a Woman* (New York: Harper and Row, 1975).

Don Williams, *The Apostle Paul and Women in the Church* (Glendale, Calif.: Regal Books, 1977).

MARRIAGE

Andre Bustanoby, *But I Didn't Want a Divorce* (Grand Rapids: Zondervan, 1978).

James Dobson, *What Wives Wish Their Husbands Knew About Women* (Wheaton, Ill.: Tyndale House, 1975).

Dennis Guernsey, *Thoroughly Married* (Waco Tex.: Word Books, 1977).

James E. Kilgore, *Try Marriage Before Divorce* (Waco, Tex.: Word Books, 1978).

Herbert J. and Fern Harrington Miles, *Husband-Wife Equality* (Old Tappan, N.J.: Revell, 1978).

Jill Renich, *To Have and to Hold* (Grand Rapids: Zondervan, 1972).

H. Norman Wright, *Communication: Key to Your Marriage* (Glendale, Calif.: Regal Books, 1979).

H. Norman Wright, *Into the High Country: Discerning God's Direction for Your Marriage* (Portland, Oreg.: Multnomah Press, 1979).

H. Norman Wright, *The Living Marriage* (Old Tappan, N. J.: Revell, 1975).

H. Norman Wright, *Pillars of Marriage* (Glendale, Calif.: Regal Books, 1979).

CHILDREN AND FAMILY

James Dobson, *Dare to Discipline* (Wheaton, Ill.: Tyndale House, 1970).

Ross Campbell, *How to Really Love Your Child* (Wheaton, Ill.: Victor Books, 1977).

Edith Schaeffer, *What Is a Family?* (Old Tappan, N. J.: Revell, 1975).

H. S. Vigeveno and Anne Claire, *Divorce and the Children* (Glendale, Calif.: Regal Books, 1979).

John White, *Parents in Pain* (Downers Grove, Ill.: InterVarsity Press, 1979).

MID-LIFE CRISIS

Jim Conway, *Men in Mid-Life Crisis* (Elgin, Ill.: David C. Cook Pub., 1978).

Joel and Lois Davitz, *Making It from Forty to Fifty* (New York: Random House, 1976).

Roger L. Gould, *Transformations* (New York: Simon and Schuster, 1978).

Daniel J. Levinson, *The Seasons of a Man's Life* (New York:

Alfred A. Knopf, Ballantine Books, 1978).

Gail Sheehy, *Passages* (New York: E. P. Dutton, Bantam Books, 1976).

EMOTIONAL/SPIRITUAL HELP

David Augsburger, *Caring Enough to Confront* (Glendale, Calif.: Regal Books, 1973).

Peter E. Gillquist, *Love Is Now* (Grand Rapids: Zondervan, 1970).

Archibald D. Hart, *Feeling Free* (Old Tappan, N. J.: Revell, 1979).

Bruce Larson, *No Longer Strangers* (Waco, Tex.: Word Books, 1976).

Alan Loy McGinnis, *The Friendship Factor* (Minneapolis: Augsburg, 1979).

John Powell, *The Secret of Staying in Love* (Niles, Ill.: Argus, 1974).

Paul L. Warner, *Feeling Good About Feeling Bad* (Waco, Tex.: Word Books, 1979).

Robert L. Wise, *When There Is No Miracle* (Glendale, Calif.: Regal Books, 1977).

Philip Yancey, *Where Is God When It Hurts?* (Grand Rapids: Zondervan, 1977).

PRAYER

E. M. Bounds, *Power Through Prayer* (Grand Rapids: Baker Book House, 1972).

Cecil Osborne, *Prayer and You* (Waco, Tex.: Word Books, 1974).

Rosalind Rinker, *Prayer: Conversing with God* (Grand Rapids: Zondervan, 1959).

Ray Stedman, *Jesus Teaches on Prayer* (Waco, Tex.: Word Books, 1975).

Corrie ten Boom, *Prayers and Promises for Everybody* (Wheaton, Ill.: Harold Shaw, 1977).

John White, *Daring to Draw Near: People in Prayer* (Downers Grove, Ill.: InterVarsity Press, 1977).

CAREER GUIDANCE

Richard Nelson Bolles, *What Color Is Your Parachute?* (San Francisco: Ten Speed, 1970, rev. 1977).

John C. Crystal and Richard N. Bolles, *Where Do I Go from Here with My Life?* (New York: Seabury, 1974).

Richard Nelson Bolles, *The Three Boxes of Life* (Berkeley, Calif.: Ten Speed Press, 1978).